A MEMOIR
OF PARTING

CAROL J. ROTTMAN

Carol J. Rottman

A MEMOIR
OF PARTING

March, 2016
For Frank & Inèke-
Thanks for befriending
our family of "Yanks" so
long ago! God has blessed
and kept us all in
life and in death.
God's peace to
you on the
journey.
With love,
Carol

PRINCIPIA
MEDIA

Principia Media, LLC
678 Front Avenue NW
Suite 256
Grand Rapids, MI 49504
www.principiamedia.com

ISBN 978-1-61485-323-7

Photo Credits:
Unless otherwise noted, all photos are from the personal library of Fritz and Carol J. Rottman

Scriptural Quotations are taken from the HOLY BIBLE, NEW INTERNATIONAL VERSION® Copyright © 1973, 1978, 1984 Biblica. Used by permission of Zondervan. All rights reserved.

The "NIV" and "New International Version" trademarks are registered in the United States Patent Office by Biblical. Use of either trademark requires the permission of Biblica.

Cover and Interior Design: Frank Gutbrod
Cover Photograph by Doug Rottman
Digital Imaging: Sherry Baribeau sherrydirk.com

19 18 17 16 15 14   7 6 5 4 3 2 1

Printed in the United States of America

All the personal essays contained in this collection chronicle events as they unfolded over three years. The vignettes remain as originally written, an unpolished account, loosely strung together of the final chapter of our story. Later, I added a few reflections in italics to clarify and extend their meaning while assembling them into this book.

I express my deepest thanks to those who have walked alongside me: to all the members of the Grand Rapids Writers; The Western Seminary Journey Group: Writing as an Act of Faith; the mature students in my Memoir Classes at Calvin Academy for Lifelong Learning; and my family of faith at Eastern Avenue Christian Reformed Church. For my family, who lovingly participated in this unfolding story, bless you. And most of all to Fritz, my lifelong encourager.

Carol Rottman

Fritz and Carol on Obama Compound in Kenya

TABLE OF CONTENTS

PREFACE

Five years ago *All Nature Sings* (Rottman, 2010) came into being. The first section may give a context to the story that follows in this book.

I married a dreamer...

Not that I knew that when attracted to him—in fact he had hidden it nicely. Nor would I have known as a young coed that a dreamer was just what I needed. In the late 50's as we studied together in the Calvin College library, I realized that Fritz was hard working, smart and funny, but also had his worries. Over time they came out: Will I make the grade in grad-school? Will I get tenure as a professor? Can we afford these house payments? But the dreamer in him also showed itself. Part of his success as a biochemist came because he could imagine some of the unknowns of how living systems worked. He was coloring outside the lines before anyone coined that phrase. Many of our adventures as a family came because he could always imagine a future beyond our present state or place.

Fritz showed a deep yearning for land and growing things, even during his early days amid the industrial paper mills that polluted the air in Muskegon, Michigan. His family lived in a very modest place hemmed in by houses on either side. But their narrow lot stretched "out back" past his mother's flower garden, the garage, dad's work shed and fenced-in vegetable garden to a ridge before a steep hill. As

Bridesmaid and finance

a kid he scuttled down the incline and explored the wilds beyond. Mature oaks and a small stream bounded his side of the "gully" from which he could see celery plants growing in the rich bottomland beyond.

So I should not have been surprised—after nine years of marriage and three children, a string of rental apartments, and his first real job—he began dreaming of a piece of land where there would be room for all of us to grow. One day he called me excitedly, "You've got to see this, Carol!" Through a colleague at Michigan State University he got a tip about some tracts of land for sale bordering the Red Cedar River— the same meandering river that runs through the campus. He fell in love with the barren piece of land close to a tree-lined stream and helped me imagine a house and garden and maybe even fruit trees and beehives. I did not protest because I had no competing dream. We bought the field. We raised our three kids on Sylvan Glen Road bounded on one side by the river and the other by railroad tracks. We cultivated most of our land into gardens and grass but, beyond the end of our dirt road, virgin woods and fields invited us to explore.

Sixteen years later, with two of our children in college, we decided to leave this place to take up work in the city of Cleveland. We couldn't have known how much we left behind; we were forced by a poor housing market to buy a house in a populated suburb with traffic racing by day and night on a one-way boulevard. The house sat on what I called a civilized acre with room for a garden after several large trees had been removed to allow for full sun. The beehives came along but didn't do well in the city perhaps because of too few blooms and too much lawn fertilizer. At first Fritz was too busy in his new job and I in graduate school to lament our lost land. But unbeknownst to me the dreamer was already imagining other land and water. He made the best of city living, with eighteen years of remarkable gardens in a park-like back yard. His dream languished until he took early retirement.

All things being equal we would have retired in Colorado—my home state which both of us loved. But our children were having children and they all lived in Michigan within a 20-mile radius, a situation most grandparents covet. So the hunt was on—a tract of land near water in rural Michigan. I must admit that my dreams, even within his parameters, have always been pint-sized. But I knew the day would come when he'd call excitedly from somewhere in Michigan saying: "You've got to see this, Carol."

(*All Nature Sings: A Spiritual Journey of Place*, p. 11-12)

Wedding — June 9, 1959

REFLECTION

Our bedroom has no drawn blinds or curtains—by our choice. Situated in the middle of a prairie with only a twinkle of light from neighbors across a small lake, there is no need for privacy. Surrounded by windows, with one left ajar, the birds wake me with song and the morning light gets me out of bed to greet each new day. At the first glimmering, I slip out, don my robe and watch the sunrise—over a cup of hot, sweet tea.

First light is my cue; the faithful beginning of a new day. Eventually Fritz realizes that I am up—and he knows where to find me—by the kitchen table, looking eastward, sitting in silence. The predictability of God's light/dark order has always been reassuring. God not only made the world but also keeps it going, sunrise after sunrise.

Within our days we discover change, uncertainty and fear in unpredictable lives. Sometimes they speed along with schedules, plans and relationships, and we assume they are "normal" and will go on and on. Then change appears—sudden and catastrophic or stealing in, unawares.

Our family has known abrupt, dramatic change as well as the slower, crawling type. As we long for stability—we don't want to believe that change is our constant companion.

This story tells of the creeping variety of change, one little hint at a time, each one subtly altering our lives. First we notice, then we name the villain and forever we accommodate its wily

Our wedding reception

*ways. We lament our losses; we try to be brave. We ask the God
of order to stay with us through messy disorder.*

O God, our help in ages past,
our hope for years to come.
Be thou our guard
while troubles last
and our eternal home.

Oh God, Our Help in Ages Past, lyrics by Isaac Watts (paraphrasing Psalm 90)

INTRODUCTION

Losing It: A Memoir of Parting

Amsterdam's Schipol Airport hums and chugs at a frantic pace—transatlantic travelers changing planes for exotic parts of the world. Loudspeakers blare orders with accented voices about gates and changes and dire warnings, "Do not leave any bag unattended." Large family groups and solitary travelers scurry down long concourses, often stopping to use currency not their own, to buy a drink or a sweet. Constant noise, motion and chaos.

The first time my husband Fritz and I passed through Schipol on our way to Kenya, we followed our friend—a seasoned traveler in this part of the world. He could bypass each garbled announcement with all the information we needed. We leaned on him and he led.

In the years that followed we became regular January travelers, on our way to do mission work through that sensory overload of an airport. Making our way more confidently, nevertheless we carefully hung together. The one place we could not go together was the WC— of course, a wall separated the two restrooms. On our fifth such trip in January of 2009 I remember asking Fritz several times to wait for me right outside the doorway when he finished— something we'd done often before.

I wasted no time and soon reemerged into the bustling hallway. No Fritz. I glanced every direction before positioning myself facing the door so I would not miss him. Five minutes, ten minutes passed as panic rose. Was he still inside? If not, could I ever find him in this crowded and confusing place? How could he find his way alone? I considered announcing his name on the loudspeaker—but with his hearing loss he might never make it out. Even if he heard his name he would not know where to go. I always kept the tickets and boarding passes with me as he depended on me to get us to the right place to catch our flight. I did not dare move from the place we parted.

My eyes bobbed back and forth searching the fast moving crowd for some sight of him. I needed a plan but could think of none. Had I imagined this scene before? Suddenly, I spotted this silver haired guy wandering nearby. The tall, lean man wearing khakis and a light blue, V-neck sweater paused at a window display, neither rushed nor anxious. Fritz!

I don't remember what words tumbled out but surely a mixture of relief and scolding. He looked surprised at my emotion. He did not realize that he had forgotten our agreement. I knew in my heart he could no longer be safe without me.

From that day onward, two fiercely independent people were forced into a relationship they never imagined; needing each other for their very well-being. The stark truth slapped me long before it hit him. Little signs, often dismissed as flukes before, added up like stones in our path ready to trip the usual harmony of our give and take marriage. It is one

Fritz and Carol in Uganda

thing to navigate a rough trail, but quite another to see its ultimate destination.

Our experience is not rare. Every day couples like us hit potholes in the road, sudden turns, impossible roadblocks and slide-offs that often make getting back home seem all but impossible.

If my decision to share this journey gives hope to just one other person, it will have been worth the effort. My prayer is that it speaks to many more, lost in situations beyond understanding. This book cannot be a roadmap—there is none. For some this disease, or others like it, will advance like a swift moving train; for others it will totter by baby steps. It can be a lonely trip. These words shared might convince you that others travel alongside.

Rottman family — 1979

Like the Schipol Airport, noise and chaos reign. On that January day, Fritz and I were just two average people who almost lost each other at the restroom while making our way to the boarding area—and through to the great beyond.

This book marks the journey Fritz and I took into the murky world of dementia. I sensed the need to keep some kind of balance as his equilibrium was slipping away. Writing has been and continues to be my means of survival—a way to make sense of troubled thoughts. As changes upset our daily lives and our relationship, I tried to express them in words. This book is a string of personal essays marking our travels—not to the exciting places we used to visit, but a more pedestrian path leading to the end of the road.

Wallets, Keys and Memory

My husband boarded the Milwaukee Clipper car ferry with his buddies on his way home from their annual pheasant-hunting trip in North Dakota. While waiting to embark, he spotted an old friend, someone both of us knew from my hometown. She and her husband were traveling to see their children and thought they would take the ferry across Lake Michigan to shorten their trip. After astonished greetings, she took Fritz aside and said without fanfare: "Curt is losing it." They didn't have time to talk, then or later, because the boat was leaving and soon Marj became very seasick in gusty weather.

The original Rottman's, 2012

When Fritz got home the story came out in bits and pieces. He could not remember our friends' names, but he told me, "You know the people we stayed with on that trip?" That was enough to help me identify the couple he was talking about. The phrase "losing it" was the main part of the conversation that stuck in Fritz's mind. Now it is lodged in mine. I emailed my friend Marj later to clarify the details. Yes, Curt was showing troubling signs: he could no longer read a map, remember times for appointments, or old friends' names.

What Marj didn't know was that Fritz was showing the same signs. "Losing it." How often have I heard that phrase used, usually in hushed voices, about people just like my husband? I'll admit to having used it to describe someone else. It is as apt as it is crude—shorthand for dementia. I have also come to know how cruel the phrase and its reality feel. Losing it—I will never use those words again when speaking of another person.

Vocabulary fails us. None of us know how to deal with, much less describe what we are seeing. Most of our age-mates fear that the same could happen to them. Many a young person has had fun making a parody of the physical changes that come with old age. There is nothing funny about lost memory. When we are young and healthy, deterioration of our bodies seems far, far away. Deterioration of our minds—unthinkable.

That is, until "it" bursts into the room. Much like my husband trying to find the words to make me understand his story, we struggle to find the words to talk about it. At first I try to pass along to my children what I see without saying what I think it might mean. They have been waiting for me to say something; they give more examples. We cannot ignore signs, but we don't find them easy to describe. Hints pile up in the room displacing everything else. We don't want to see what we see.

At first the signs are unclear—all of us lose things now and then. But then I hear a call from the other room, "Carol, have you seen my wallet? I just had it but it is gone! I need to go and buy some things for the garden." So I look in the logical places and then press him for details of the last time he had it. None are forthcoming, so I mentally trace his movements since the last time he might have used the wallet. Finally I find it in the cubbyhole in our closet, perhaps removed from his back pocket when changing clothes. He looks relieved and races for the door. Soon he is back searching for his keys.

The first time he needs my help to locate something it feels normal, even routine. But day-by-day the pattern emerges—many tasks that once were second nature become harder. He relies on me to help him find things. He needs someone to pair names with people or fill in the details of his old, familiar stories.

People like me live alongside a spouse or parent or child and experience changes as they accumulate and become a fact of life. We are powerless to change things—powerless to get away—powerless to express.

But—I have to try, for my sake. Self-preservation is my selfish goal. So I will struggle to tell our story without a clue about where the plot is going. I'm writing to find out what I'm thinking. No two people see illness, change, and life the same way or talk about it with the same words. Still, I believe that the experience of one can sometimes shine a light on the experiences of many. Knowing that many feel a similar sense

Carol among wildflowers on prairie

of loss watching persons they love decline, is enough to push me forward. I'm hoping that together we may also find some surprising joy.

Frederick Buechner once asked, when writing about his life, "Who cares? What in the world could be less important than who I am…the bad times, the good times, the moments of grace?"

He goes on to answer his question:

"…I talk about my life anyway because if, on the one hand, hardly anything could be less important, on the other *hand, hardly anything could be more important. My story is important not because it is mine, God knows, but because if I tell it anything like right, the chances are you will recognize that in many ways it is also yours.*

Maybe nothing is more important than that we keep track, you and I, of these stories of who we are and where we have come from and the people we have met along the way because it is precisely through these stories in all their particularity, as I have long believed and often said, that God makes himself known to each of us most powerfully and personally. If this is true, it means that to lose track of our stories is to be profoundly impoverished not only humanly but spiritually."

from *Telling Secrets*, Harper Collins, 1991

YESTERDAY

Young Fritz with a collie dog in the backfield

FIRST LIGHT OF DAWN

Remembering for Two

The appetites of pregnant women are notorious. From pickles at midnight to ice cream for breakfast, husbands often indulge this fickle eater for two. I was that person during three pregnancies more than forty years ago. My husband teased, scolded, and pampered me until each baby came and my overeating was replaced by overfeeding the little one. He played his part but happily gave it up when the nutrition crisis was over.

Over the years of marriage that now number fifty plus, we have each tried to supply what the other lacked during challenging times. He stood beside me when I contended with a sudden and lengthy bout of internal bleeding, flying with me to the Mayo Clinic and taking up residence in Rochester for over a month while I recovered. I nursed him back to health from serious illnesses that included prostate cancer and kidney failure, the latter resulting in a transplant. Each physical ill led to gradual improvement and a slow return of independence. Both the patient and the partner worked toward that day—the hope of which provided a measure of patience even in stressful situations. "You *will* get better," was the promise at the end of the rainbow. Time after time we have found that pot of gold and have gone on to enjoy more normal days.

Several years ago our good friend was diagnosed with ALS, a degenerative disease also know as Lou Gehrig's disease. His wife, who had been one of my closest friends when we lived in the same town, accepted the challenge—knowing full well that he would never get better. She found in-home care, sought new ways to make his altered life more comfortable, and helped him continue his work until he could no longer communicate. Even though their adult children lived a distance away, the two sons and a daughter divided the weekends and came so their dad would have family care when his attendant was off. Their loving care was unwavering even as he traveled the rocky road of deterioration and finally death.

My friend's devotion came to mind last week as my husband prepared for the annual hunting trek to North Dakota. Fritz's brother, Jack, had been part of the group for many years, but had to drop out permanently because of complications after back surgery. As we packed my husband's hunting clothes and equipment, we both began to wonder if this year might be his last as well.

Organizing seemed more difficult; he made lists, lost them, and made new lists. An old habit of "getting his house in order" before leaving, became an obsession for him and he transferred more to me. The garden, his desk, the home upkeep pressed on him, as if everything needed his final instructions before parting.

I neglected my own work and stayed available to relieve his frustration. On the day that he scolded me for dropping a little sand from a basil plant onto the garage floor he had just swept,

Fritz with a mess of trout in Marble, 1960

I knew we were in trouble. His usual mild-mannered ways were giving way to sudden flashes of anger. He berated my sloppiness; he could not let it go. His old perfectionist habits were asserting themselves even as he rushed to get ready. The day before leaving, he worked too long, meticulously weeding a garden that would soon freeze, and fell into the recliner, exhausted. I wondered not only about his judgment but also about his stamina for the hunt. In years past he would begin walking considerable distances just to build up endurance for those long days traversing the fields. Not this year.

So I sent him off with a wish and a prayer. That first day of his absence I was exhausted. I had been unable to sleep the night before his departure as days of working with him and combating his worries on top of my own took their toll. We had reviewed over and over the details of what to bring and what needed to be accessible during the long van ride. I suddenly realized that I was becoming his memory. Once he was safely in the company of his long-time friend, I rested and returned to my usual writing and teaching.

Finally, I felt the weight lifting as I only had to remember for one.

I worked for many years with young children, my own and those I taught, all dependent in some way. I firmly believed in requiring them to do as much for themselves as possible. For their sake and mine, I did not want to be an enabler. It is so much easier for the weak to latch onto the strong than to do things that seem hard.

When did I become the memory crutch for my husband? Was it the first time he searched for the name of someone he had known for years? Was it when his anxiety at going to an important meeting almost paralyzed him, and I stood by the door checking for items he should have with him that day? Was it when he made a financial error, and we had to redo a year of taxes or when I realized that routine use of the computer agitated him?

At first, I pushed him like I would a child. I tried to think of memory jogs for him. I reviewed some details, like meeting schedules, but he still relied on me to get him there on time. At one point I urged him to travel to Cleveland without me for a meeting—until his panic set in and I reluctantly agreed to go. I tried to simplify life with notes on a white board on the fridge until he decided it looked childish. I urged him to play the memory games that I enjoy. He thought it was a nice idea—for some later day.

One day I caught myself scolding him for some elementary lapse. I was ashamed. The truth was emerging. Like my friend facing her husband's ALS, I was facing something progressive—relentlessly progressive. In the same way she did, I had to realize there was no turning back. Her husband deteriorated physically; my husband was losing his memory—the memory that helped him become a brilliant scientist, remembering complex DNA structures and citations in journals from decades ago. Now his conversations among other molecular biologists were about safer subjects: gardens and weather. The memory that never forgot an important date or a detail of home or car maintenance had given way to worry over the date of the last oil change and how much pressure the tires need. His was the memory I had come to rely on as he went about his day-to-day tasks independently, just as I went about mine.

Now, with a week of reprieve, I realize a painful truth: I have been remembering for two.

I cannot ignore the daily reminders, the signs that appear when I least expected them: a little sand, anger at his computer, trouble packing a suitcase. These changes are not like craving ice cream at breakfast, which will pass with the birth of a child. Memory loss has no nine-month, end-of-term relief. I know in my heart that all the games, memory jogs and repeated details will not lead to improvement. All signs point in only one direction.

There are song lyrics that tell our story: "You have to be there, you <u>have to</u> be there…"* If my new role is to remember for both of us, I must stay beside him. I will keep safe all that he is losing and become our memory bank. We saved

Otter Cove, Canada — about 1970

those memories together but now I am the only one who can withdraw from our account.

* You Have to Be There, sung by Susan Boyle on her album, Someone to Watch over Me. Bjorn Ulvaeus (lyrics) and Benny Anderson (music)

10/2010

Stealing Monday

I love Mondays—always have. It may be my favorite day. Sunday is a close second because it paves the way for Monday. After a Sunday of worship, reflection, and reading—anything but work—I am ready to go. The dawn of a Monday always ushers in a burst of pent-up energy and eagerness. Rest brings peace; work brings satisfaction.

This week someone stole Monday. He moaned: poor sleep, feelings of "not good," "I don't know what's wrong." I am not sure if his complaints are physical or emotional, but I suspect he cannot face the drudgery of his desk, the place that had always been his haven.

I try to save Monday from his frequent interruptions and glum predictions. All his talk of "can't do," "nothing is going right," and "I wasted the whole day" robbed me of Monday joy. Unhappy with himself, he is unhappy with me. He insists that he doesn't blame me, but my attempts at cheer are rebuffed.

Early afternoon he agitates to go to the gym, our winter pattern for exercise. He misses working outside now that the weather is cool and no garden chores remain. Working at the desk is no longer satisfying, as it just reminds him of all the things that no longer bring pleasure, like answering email from friends and reading *Science* magazine from cover to cover. So we head for the gym before I have even begun Monday's work. It is the only way he can work out his restlessness.

After a few rounds of walking briskly on the track, his tension slips away. He goes next to his usual routine on the weight machines, pushing himself to do the prescribed number of repeats. After the workout, we stop at Jody's, a restaurant in nearby Rockford, for a bowl of chili. We talk about his morning discouragement and the help he needs to organize his life.

The day is reclaimed; he even returns to his desk after the evening news. We set a date for Wednesday, when I will join him in his basement study to discover the things that block progress. He has always had a sense of order—close to perfectionism. My order is different, but he must be in charge.

I can't reclaim Monday with its lost labors. It is gone like so many solitary hours and days I once enjoyed. I lament the books unread and the stories unwritten. Most of all, I lament the man who is slipping away from me as we try to restore some predictability in his life. I must listen and learn without imposing my style on his.

In the past we were on equal footing, simply acknowledging our differences and living within them. Now I must be so careful not to rock his already unsteady sense of self. I hold back my usual impulses. No teasing, sparring, laughing at foibles, his or my own. This is serious business.

This Monday revealed to me that I have a new assignment; to walk through all days with him just as they come, not wishing for those good old Mondays.

11/2010

Alaska with Grandson Matt

Soaring into the Unknown

A day comes every fall when winter is in the air. All denial, based on unseasonably balmy days and abundant sunshine, disappears into gray skies and damp air. It has nothing to do with official dates; those of us who live close to nature, just know. On Sunday my husband urged me to take our usual afternoon walk, but one glance out the window gave me the chills. Not to be shamed by my preference for warm and cozy, I bundled up. We avoided the woods when we heard shots from hunters practicing for opening day. Looking over the lake from the dock we spotted a large bird gliding through the steely sky—an eagle.

Fritz with fish caught in our back yard on the Red Cedar River (1968)

High above us, the splendid bird gave us a show. Slight variations in hue shaded the sky so that as the eagle soared and floated on the wind currents it was, at times, more visible. Its movements were so carefree and playful. Shivering from the cold breeze, I would have been more comfortable walking briskly, but I could not take my eyes away from the bird. I wanted to hold onto something no photograph could portray: the shine that elegant bird brought to my spirit on the day I knew, from my head down to my boots, that winter had come.

And He will raise you up on eagle's wings,
Bear you on the breath of dawn,
Make you to shine like the sun,
And hold you in the palm of His Hand.

Michael Jonas, 1979 – "On Eagle's Wings"

I wrote the above as a blog post several days before I knew something else in my bones. I had been trying to ignore its coming as much as winter's chill. Several times on that Wednesday, while my husband and I were working closely together on consolidating files from both of our studies, I had mentioned my plan to drive across town to transport our son, who is in a wheelchair and does not drive, to an appointment. I kept the time in mind but was soon overwhelmed by the task of moving the financial files to my office. Fritz's study is on the lower level and mine on the second floor so I carried lots of stuff up to my room. I became engulfed in the minutia of reorganizing and merging important files so I could find them easily. The time got away from me. I quickly went downstairs to say goodbye. My husband was just answering the phone, so I said, "I've got to go. Call me on my cell phone."

Much later, after my transporting was done, having received no call, I rang Fritz to see if he had gone to workout at the gym and to tell him when I would be home. He was angry: "Where have you been? Why did you have to leave so fast?" In his mind I had simply left with no explanation. I listened and tried to be calm when telling him of what had taken me from the house. After hearing his accusations, I said I would be home with supper, just a little late. Driving home enclosed within my little car, I could feel it heavy on my heart and my bones. With this knowing, there was no eagle soaring.

When I walked in, he asked in an accusing voice, "Where were you?" I just looked at him. He really did not know! I put my arms around him. "Your memory," I cried. I did not have to say more. At that moment I realized not only that his short-term memory loss was real but also that it would have a devastating impact on our lives together.

He had a flash of understanding, leading to a look of despair. He paced round and round the kitchen, not knowing what to do. And then he told me that he would volunteer for any experimental treatment that might help, even if it could kill him. Such strong feelings.

I was unsure whether he could feel how his memory loss would affect me. Going forward, I can't assume he will remember plans, even those within that day. I must double-check often; stay closer to home. For the first time, I sensed the kind of "bearing up" we are going to need.

I remembered the eagle, soaring and gliding. It looked so easy for him just to let the wind currents come from below and carry him. I wanted to trust that God's wings would lift both Fritz and me to see the light of every dawn, even through each day's shadows. A shining sun seemed remote on a cold and windy Sunday, but gray days don't last forever.

On this day, being held in God's hands seemed as remote as that eagle in the sky when I realized that Fritz forgot where I was. But God promised.

Those whose hope is in the Lord will renew their strength
They will soar on wings like eagles (Isaiah 4:31a).

I must hang on to that.

11/2010

Finding My Way Back Home

Soon after they returned from the hunting trip, Fritz announced he had been invited to go deep-sea fishing with his friend. I was happy that his hunting/fishing buddy had invited him to go, even knowing that he would have to keep an eye out for his friend—until I learned that they had to leave for Mexico on the afternoon of Thanksgiving. Fritz committed to the trip without asking me.

The days before Thanksgiving, when I usually shop, clean and bake pies, were interrupted by his confusion of schedule, what to bring and what the airlines would allow. We rehearsed the details because he was used to leaning on me while traveling. I trusted his longtime colleague and friend, Loran, to do my usual part and shepherd Fritz along with the group. On the morning of the holiday, just before our family arrived, I was amazed to see Fritz's change of clothes, his packed bag and his passport stowed in a backpack, on the side of the bedroom for easy access.

He laughed and talked during our large Thanksgiving gathering, as if he hadn't a care in the world. He neither offered help in the dinner prep or setting up tables for seventeen, nor

Deep sea fishing

did I ask him for any. He asked me to do his usual prayer before the meal, relieving him of a common source of stress. Just after four o'clock I signaled that he needed to get ready to go. We conferred one last time about where certain things were in his bags. Then he said his good-byes to the children, grandchildren and the friends who were sharing the feast. I followed Fritz into the garage to give him a private hug.

"I hope I can find my way back home," he said with a mischievous grin. Loran, the organizer and handler of details was fully aware of his role in making the trip work for Fritz; it was his idea. Since their years together as biochemistry professors at Michigan State University, they had enjoyed trips for pheasant hunting for over thirty years and two trips fishing in Alaska. Loran and I didn't have to talk about the changes in his friend—he experienced them. Maybe his thoughts echoed mine: "Just one last trip?"

I imagined Fritz, caught up within this group of fishermen, following their experienced leader—all with the same agenda: catch big fish in the ocean! In years past each of us had taken trips without the other, several times a year— refreshing "spaces in our togetherness," that always made reunions at home so joyful. Could this trip mark the end of distant travel in general? Could it be the prelude to concern of even near travel to the neighborhood gas station alone?

In some ways, Fritz was not aware of his dependence. I tried not to let on that I had become more parent than partner. Loran would spare me the details of his concerns for Fritz while on this fishing trip. He would glow, as always, in the flush of an invigorating time, when he finally returned with Fritz.

And I would congratulate my fisherman, with a warm hug for finding his way back home to me.

11/30/10

Grandpa showing his catch to the kids

A Diagnosis

Ever since his kidney transplant in 2005, Fritz had been required to have his blood tested periodically. After each visit we were reassured that his blood work was okay. One morning after an early blood draw and appointment with his doctor, Fritz came home with a white appointment slip. It listed the name of a doctor but not the type of clinic. When I quizzed him, he told me a sketchy story. His usual doctor was not there that morning and when the physician's assistant, who he had seen often before, asked him some questions, he stumbled. "I told her I was having 'memory issues.' So she told me she wanted me to see another doctor." I put down the appointment on our calendar like I had so many before.

The day of this added appointment came and when we walked into the medical suite the name surprised us, "Alzheimer's Clinic." This was to be a screening! After all my wondering about the troubling signs I'd seen, and questioning how one finds out if a condition is really dementia, here we were. "Not to worry," said the doctor, "this is just a preliminary, quick review of your functioning." He wanted me to be present. He tested the usual things—remember three words, put hands and numbers on a clock face and draw some shapes—that my mother reported long ago were the classic tests to see "if you were crazy." I watched in disbelief, first that we were actually there and then how Fritz responded. The tests were not at all quick, involving checking reflexes and responding to rapid commands. When the doctor was finished he dismissed us with a cheery, "I'll be sending a report."

Fritz after Kidney transplant in 2005

Fritz was tired as we drove home. We both knew he had not done well. But we went on with our daily lives wondering if this test had verified what we already suspected. No report came.

Months later I met a woman whose husband had just been diagnosed with vascular dementia and she talked about the testing and treatment he received. She talked about the drugs her husband was taking that could slow the process. I should have known that if Fritz were diagnosed he might get some treatment. Only then did I check back with the clinic to find out why we had not gotten a report. I learned that the results were sent to Fritz's doctors not to us. If they had told Fritz the results and he failed to tell me, I would have understood. I don't think they did. Both doctors had been his students when studying biochemistry as premed students. Perhaps they didn't want to believe that this was happening to their mentor. I finally received our copy of the four-page report with its results couched in medical terminology. One finding caught my eye; Fritz was successfully compensating for his memory loss because of his innate intelligence. The word Alzheimer's was not used.

Meanwhile, short-term memory and word loss became Fritz's daily burden. Feeling letdown by the first doctor, I searched for another clinic to do the testing. Soon after Fritz's trip to Mexico, he spent a half day doing a battery of tests with four different professionals. I witnessed all but the neuropsychological exam. Again he was tired and convinced that he had done poorly. One of the doctors told us that they would call in about a week when the results were ready, and we could come in for a consultation.

However, soon after we got home, the clinic called to see if we could come in the next day for the report. During the interviews I mentioned that we were slated to return to Kenya in January for about a month and wondered to myself if there might be a reason we should not go.

It was a gray, December day when two members of the team delivered the results patiently and clearly; "symptoms consistent with Alzheimer's." The kind way that they delivered the news made it feel less like Fritz had "flunked" the tests and more that the testing made things clearer.

The news was not a surprise to either of us. In some strange way it was a relief to finally name the "it" that had invaded our home and left us both so unsteady. The doctors urged us to travel to Kenya anyway. We continued with plans for our trip, knowing full well it would be our last.

I am not sure this diagnosis was the turning point for us. But it changed our fears into facts, at least as factual as medical knowledge can decipher without an autopsy. No more wishing that the signs were imaginary and might go away. Dementia was now part of our lives—the one that both of us will live together with no end in sight.

12/10/10

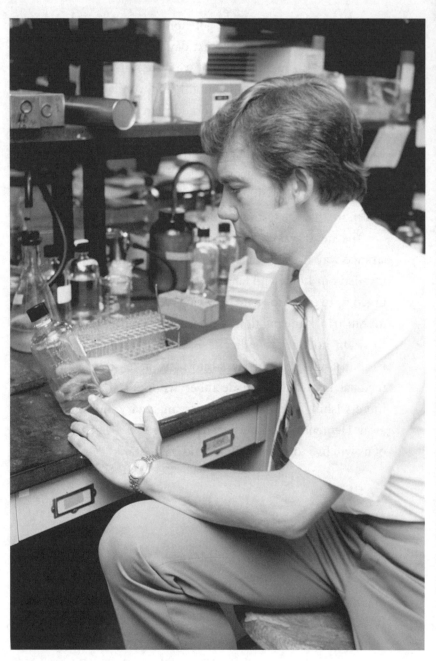

Fritz the researcher at MSU

CHAPTER TWO

IN THE LIGHT OF DAY

Reflection

Dementia brought "inequality" into our marriage. So many things that my husband had always done, he could no longer do. There was a large binder in his study of the hundreds of published scientific papers he had written. Years of income tax returns filled the cabinets, which he had done without any help from me. He carefully organized his workroom, office and garage and let me know if I didn't keep up his orderly ways. He had been the wise negotiator, the caring friend and decisive decision maker. He had a talent for visualizing space, making it functional and pleasing to the eye.

Like a thief who came not one night, but every night to get something of value, Alzheimer's stole little by little. I had to compensate for the lost skills, often proving to be a poor substitute. One thing the thief could not take was Fritz's honesty about having and coping with his disease. Whenever able, he bravely took the lead.

Can a healthy mind ever fathom the alienation a person feels when the body and mind you depend on are letting you down? We expect some physical limitations with age but we depend on the brain to be the master controller. If some bodily part does not work, the brain tells us how to compensate. If a physical problem is serious there are many repair-persons eager to put us together again. But if the control center falters, it is a Humpty Dumpty matter—who will put the egg back together?

Searching for Words

"Have you seen the _____?" I hear from upstairs and come right away, knowing that searching upsets him.

"You know, the thing from the bank," he says as he tries to show with his hands how large it is.

"Do you mean the bank card?"

"No. The blue thing we've got so many of."

"The bank statement?"

He gestures again, now a little frustrated that I do not understand. "You know." I don't. But I watch his hands once more holding his hands apart the distance of about a foot.

I'm puzzled but I keep guessing, trying not to raise my voice. All of a sudden I think of the blue pens that he likes which come from our bank. "Pens?"

"Yes."

"Oh, honey," I say and give him a knowing hug. He knows and I know that the one piece of information, the noun that would anchor the search to a known object—is missing. The question, the gesturing and the guessing games that follow go on until I make a connection with clues he gives.

"We used to have so many. Where have they all gone?" he says, rushing on to be about his business. It leaves me wondering just how long he will go through all this hassle just to find something. I wonder how long I will be able to relieve his frustration by coming up with the word that eludes him.

I am surprised that nouns are the first things to go. When a child begins to talk, nouns are the first words spoken: ball, house, bed. After naming the object, other words can be added, like, "I want the____" or "my _____." I recall how triumphant our children were when they realized that naming things was a key to communication. People listened. People understood. Adding other words made their desires even clearer. But without the initial noun, listeners must rely on gestures for clues. Usually for little children, the object is in sight and therefore reaching or pointing helps. But for adults, who can no longer bring out the words they want when they want them, the challenge is greater. You expect that of babies but not of grown men.

The word search began with proper names: not being able to think of the names of the people he had talked to at church and wanting to tell me about their conversations. These were not new acquaintances, some, friends for years. He could generally remember what they talked about, even though he relayed the conversation out of sequence, leaving me to piece together fragments to form a whole story. If I discovered the person first, then I could usually understand the thread of their interaction.

Relaying a telephone conversation is becoming difficult. Today he has a private conversation with our son. The content upset him but he cannot explain why. With his permission I sometimes listen in so that I know what was said instead of having to rely on his reiteration.

I spend lots of time with word puzzles—too much, I think sometimes. He expresses displeasure when I get wrapped up in the game. But learning to understand him is a totally different type of puzzle: find the missing word—not the one that fits but the one he acts out.

Years ago, I had some success with teaching blind preschool kids who struggled with language development.

Spartan fan with gift pumpkin

Without sight, naming objects was difficult. Slowly, pairing one object with one word, they built their vocabulary.

I want to learn the skill of deciphering language, not as it is developing but declining. I want so much more: to understand his deepest thoughts—to share the things that are inside. How does it feel to see what you want or know what you want to say, and not be able to find words? Someday will his actions have to speak without words? Wordless, will he be same person?

My deepest fear is that a time will come when all language will be lost.

2/2011

The Spiral

It is eight o'clock in the morning; I am worried. I have sent Fritz off alone for an early morning, routine blood test followed by a doctor's visit, even after I decided three weeks ago I should go with him to all appointments from now on. He insisted my coming was unnecessary. I should have realized that his judgment, even in simple matters, is compromised. But I was tired after a demanding and emotional day and welcomed the chance just to stay at home and find some peace. So I let him go. Now peace eludes me. I can do nothing but wonder if Fritz is managing alone.

A few days ago he began a new medication, replacing one of the antirejection drugs he takes to protect his transplanted kidney. The former had been implicated in "memory loss" so the doctor, upon hearing of Fritz's problem with memory, decided to try an alternative. The new drug's warnings sound ominous, especially "confusion," which is precisely the problem he is facing.

Confusion that called me urgently on the desk intercom one day. I rushed down to find him nearly paralyzed in his thinking while he tried to work at his desk. He could not find, and still cannot find, the packet of papers with monthly investment reports that I brought to him several days before. He tried to write his appointments on his computer calendar and got completely confused. "I feel like I am spiraling downward," he said. I watched over a period of several days: he could not enter what he wanted; my instruction did not lead to new learning; later, he went in again and messed it up. He hoped the date plus notes would serve as his memory. He desperately wanted to "keep things straight," as he said, "but they just get more crooked."

Last night he asked me to review the blood draw process again. This morning he was still unclear about which paper to take and the times of both appointments. I tried to keep it simple, "White paper to lab. After the draw, go upstairs to the transplant office."

Just now he called from the hospital, wanting to know the next step after the blood draw, which he has routinely done since his transplant almost six years ago. Why did I let him go alone? Alone, his problems will be all the more evident to the staff. How will I know what the doctor says? It is time that I do the things I know I should even though he says they are not necessary. It is time for me to deal with today's reality, even though the future seems unsettled and the past beyond recovery.

My prayers were for a slow unfolding of Fritz's condition but instead dementia has rushed in. So recently, I felt strong and resourceful but now guess and second-guess everything. We are not in "free-fall," but confusion reigns. Like my lifelong partner, I feel like my downward spiral has begun. How soon will we hit the bottom?

2/11/11

Telling Friends

When does one deliver the news: "I have Alzheimer's?"

Hopefully never, but in Fritz's case the time had come. First, he told our kids—made a date with each one and had a talk. They were not noticeably shocked. Earlier they had seen and commented to me about his repeating and not being able to come up with the intended word. I had also kept them informed about the steps we were taking to understand his situation better. Once they heard "I have Alzheimer's," from his mouth, they stood beside him in a new way, showering him with love.

What a relief when he could say the A-word to our children and their spouses and explain as much as he knows of what is happening to him. If the unknowns were confusing to us in his circle, imagine how upsetting they must be for him to slowly lose his bearings. Now that the adults all know: we can talk freely among ourselves. We are the ones who love each other no matter what.

He asked the adults not to talk about it with their kids just yet. We chose not to spread the circle of knowing, because they might treat him differently. Fritz has always been concerned about how he is perceived by others, even dressing conservatively so that he does not stand out in a crowd. He often took the back seat, reserving his opinions for when or if the time was right.

During testing and the counseling that followed his diagnosis, Fritz was urged to let go of things that cause stress. Since retiring in 1999, he has maintained positions on several boards—one with a local research institute and one with the medical school of which he was a part for eighteen years. During the last year his anxiety has risen sharply before every meeting day, to the point of near immobilization. Matters being considered were too complicated, the conversations too fast moving and his contributions very limited. His anxiety was mainly prompted by the fear of saying or doing something that would draw unwanted attention.

One such incident did occur. A group of trustees and executives were gathered to discuss a topic. Several persons were invited as guests to add to their discussion. During a

Chris and Fritz hunting pheasant

routine, "Let's introduce ourselves," Fritz was unable to speak when it was his turn. As he tells the story, he opened his mouth and nothing came out. Someone graciously supplied his information and the introductions continued. He was mortified. His already shaky self-confidence worsened.

These board positions were his last link to a science community, like those in which he had thrived for his whole career. As much as he disliked the meetings and all the high-level glitz of their social affairs, he enjoyed the status. It gave him the credential that he lost when he retired from university teaching. "Emeritus" sounds so "has-been," he once said.

This week was a turning point. Getting ready for a meeting was painful, with materials to download from a website, which he cannot do alone. He requested paper copies but that necessitated a trip to the institute he served. While there he talked to several people who sought his council about some personnel matters as a member of the board's "arbitration committee." He had no memory of his appointment and no desire to serve. "I felt so foolish," he said. We both knew the time had come for him to make a graceful exit.

Anticipating the "why" questions if he resigned, he decided to make a lunch date with two colleagues who knew the inner workings of the institute and with whom he could entrust his news. He spent the whole morning rehearsing what he would say and how he would say it. His anxiety rose. He sought my advice. I wrote out a list of the items he had mentioned. At one point he wanted me to go with him, which I was willing to do. In the end he chose to head out alone.

I waited and worried. The meeting time came; I could not concentrate. In my imagination he was struggling to get his words out and be clear about his mission. But some things I just had to let go, especially when feeling powerless.

He was gone too long—at least it felt that way. I spent lots of time trying to concentrate on making a complicated supper, all the while waiting to hear the garage door opening. Finally he arrived—looking calmer than at any time during the day. "They were wonderful!" His friends offered to simplify his leaving.

He could not relay the conversation clearly, but he showed me just how important this first step was on his journey. His friends received him as they always had, with love and understanding, just like family. He asked them to share the information only with their spouses for now, but it was clear the circle of knowing had enlarged.

Today Fritz began the very hardest part—saying: "I have Alzheimer's." It made me so proud of him. He was brave; I wanted to have a brave heart too.

2/25/11

Joining the Savvy Creative Caregiving Group

Strangers sit behind several tables and introductions begin at our first gathering of women living with people who have dementia. One thing we share: We are or will become caregivers.

I readily admit to the group that the word "caregiver" causes me discomfort because it doesn't seem to fit. I am my husband's companion and his wife. Despite all I do for or with him, I have never called it "care." Our marriage is one of loving and respecting. Both of us have taken on those expectations voluntarily.

Caregiver is not a role that suits me. As time passes and his brain continues to change, can I assume the title? And more importantly, can he accept the role of "care-receiver?"

The group leaders stress that caregiving is a job, or more precisely a complex set of tasks requiring the skills of CEO, nurse, social director and administrator. Over the last few years I have assumed various tasks that we previously shared or that Fritz handled alone. Each time it was based on concern by one of us that he might make a mistake with medicine or taxes or important appointments. At first it seemed only natural that I begin to do what he had always done for me: save me from tasks I hated or he was better at doing. Then it hit: the balance had shifted. The kind of work I was taking

In the high country

on required complicated thinking, planning, and most of all remembering. In short: caregiving.

The seven women in our caregiver's group are all more experienced and perhaps more savvy than me. When they share their stories of caring for their mothers or their husbands I begin to see what "care" looks like. One woman asserts she has been a caregiver all her married life. Another tells of her husband, earlier diagnosed with PTSD, now graduating to dementia. A daughter describes caring for her mother, while at the same time experiencing her own forgetfulness in the aftermath of surgery. She wants to learn how to care for herself as well as her mother, while dealing with many unresolved mother-daughter issues.

As the leader repeats often, "If you have met one person with Alzheimer's, you have met one person with Alzheimer's. No two are alike and no family is built the same way." You have to plan ahead, the teachers say, for what is coming. Each person here is on a separate path: we can empathize but we cannot share a fail-safe way to get through this. All routes will not be the same, even though they will all turn in the same direction.

The changes my husband is experiencing and I am witnessing have come gradually, one reason that seeking a diagnosis was difficult. Incremental changes are not always evident to people living together for many years. The first to note change are people we see infrequently, like tax accountants and relatives from other states. But even if I, or one of my children, notice subtle differences in behavior, it is hard to name them or talk about them.

Several years ago I read a friend's book about his wife's decline. The day he realized that she had dementia was the day she dressed for church on Tuesday. Mine was less dramatic: Fritz had always offered the prayer before holiday dinners when we gathered with the children and grandchildren. Ever since subbing for him on Thanksgiving, he asked me to take over the job that had always been his. Before this, I had never thought of praying in my husband's place as caregiving.

Every woman in the group has come to realize that the care offered now is the beginning of much more to come. None of us wants to look ahead very far. We all know dementia is progressive and not reversible; we just don't know how it will unfold in our homes—how it will look on the face of the person we love. Gradually more care will be needed, some of which will test every instinct a wife or daughter has for her husband or parent. We are told that at some point loving will

Distinguished Alumni at Calvin college—2008

convert to pure commitment—staying with the job long after reaching the limit of talent and endurance.

I have never been able to visualize the interior of a new house, and now cannot imagine my familiar home run by a caregiver, even if I am that person. The setting will not change, only our togetherness in that place. My mind's eye visualizes a teeter-totter that can no longer go up and down and rest in the middle because of equal weight. I see one side up, one side down—stuck in place.

I long to greet each new stage with creativity and problem-solving but doubt it will feel savvy. In the past Fritz and I met every challenge together. Can I adapt and accommodate? The losses from dementia are his alone; caring with all my heart cannot recover even one of them. I want to shield him from seeing the sadness in my eyes—my own loss of him inch by inch.

I am a caregiver-in-training yet resist the title and new profession. Running away is no option. The two of us became "we" so long ago that I do not know how to operate except in tandem. Fritz cares *for* me even as he needs more *from* me. One of us may lead a little more now, but while we are a couple, neither of us will ever walk alone.

3/25/11

Troubles Come in Bundles

Troubles come in bundles, the old saying goes. In my experience if they are big troubles the bundle feels less like a backpack and more like a millstone hanging around my neck. I try to find some way to remove it by using every power to solve problems, one-by-one, and get on with life. There was a time in my life when troubles seemed heavy. One of our children was seriously injured just as we were in the process of moving to Cleveland to begin a new job for my husband and graduate school for me. We took up residence in a house, a neighborhood and a community that were totally foreign. Our middle child, a son, remained in the hospital and then rehab for almost a year, while our family tried to regroup, with one child away in college and another struggling to adjust to a new high school.

Looking back at that time more than thirty years ago, it is hard to believe that we survived the weight. I was younger then, much more resilient and full of energy. Most importantly, I did not have to figure everything out alone. Even though Fritz began a new, very demanding job, we always talked over the concerns that needed decisions. Our injured son could no longer move anything below his chest, but his mental powers were sharp allowing him to problem-solve and move toward independence—despite all his losses. Our daughters pitched in even while they were in the middle of their own particular challenges. Old friends prayed from afar, and we made new friends at church and work. One-by-one each problem found a solution, or at least a way for us to get by it and move on. Slowly we adjusted to our altered lives; the millstone seemed lighter. We even felt some satisfaction that we had endured.

Today's bundle of troubles feels different. The assaults are less physical and more psychological. My rock of a husband can no longer be an equal partner in decisions large or small. After repeating the same set of facts more than once, I wonder if it is wise to include him. In a group discussion of an idea or challenge he gets lost but sticks to his talking points, whether or not they fit into the flow of the discussion. His head spins at the pace of speech especially when a discussion gets heated.

Over the years Fritz and I argued over thorny questions, equally ready to use our powers of persuasion in good, fair fights. Together we hammered out similar troubles, like those that surround us today. We alternately pushed and pulled in a tug-of-war until we found a way to move ahead. I never really prized that partnership until it went missing. Now his mental health changes all that.

The other man in our lives is son, Doug. He chose social work as his profession, completing college and grad school after he became a quadriplegic at seventeen. After the first intense months of worry over his survival, we watched him deal with his new life. My husband and I worked to stay in the background as he found his way, but stood by when he

Fritz the professor

needed us. Knowing his obvious dependence on others for help, I realized how important it was to keep my motherly distance so he could fully mature. We kept close by letter and call. He settled in Michigan, found a job and maintained a household with some roommates. He met the woman he would marry. Both of us felt some sadness at letting go of our closeness but so thankful to God that he could have a "normal" life with his wife.

He has always been my listening ear and gave me those little nudges that a mom needs when she doubts her abilities. In the last few months, I have felt the loss of my other main supporter. Now he needs me in ways he has not for many years and has less energy to empathize with my losses because of his own. His marriage ended. He had grown comfortable with the life they built together with their three children, and could not imagine living without them. Our whole family rallied to stand by him just as we always had.

Again double troubles weigh me down. Two strong men in my life are facing challenges none of us ever imagined. When the Alzheimer's diagnosis came for my husband, I did not fall apart thinking I could handle it. But now with frequent doctor visits and a confusing drug regimen for Fritz and Doug's needs, I am less sure. At times like these when I would like to lean on them, I am the one leaned upon. By default, I must be the leader. The new role is mine whether I understand it, am ready or prepared.

The leaders of that caregiver's course stressed—take care of yourself. Those strong warnings come to mind every time I give up my walk for another kind of work. My need to write, a passion that always revives me, is now complicated with distractions and unfinished business. The pressure of doing things that don't come naturally, weighs on me. Sometimes I eat on the run, barely tasting the fast food. Today, I admitted to my son that the forty-five minute drive to his house that used to be a burden now is a wonderful island of quiet time. Turning off the radio and practicing deep breathing, I focus on one thing—not many.

One fact from the class I will not forget: caregivers often die before the person they care for. In dementia—the loss of mental powers seldom taxes the body. But working to keep that person safe, occupied, clean and happy—does. The effects can be lethal.

3/29/11

Prairie wildflower

CHAPTER THREE

SEARCHING FOR MORE LIGHT

Early Stage Dementia Support Group

I knew this was something we had to do. My friend told me it worked well for her and her husband so I talked to Fritz about going. I was surprised that he was eager to learn more and be among people like him who were facing the same issues. We were carefully screened by phone and then a "live interview." Finally we were in. The first session is tomorrow and as I write out Dementia Support, I recoil. I hate the word dementia; I hate the word Alzheimer's. When writing it in a letter I just put AZ, which could just as well stand for Alcatraz.

Last night I spoke to a woman who attended a talk that I gave about my book, *All Nature Sings*. She told of a mutual friend "who is really bad." Translation: she has dementia and is getting less able each day. But she stays in her house with a full-time live-in helper, because her late husband made sure she would never have to leave. "It is so sad," she said and I nod. To hear of people like him with dementia saddens me— the same reaction that our friends have or will have when they learn about Fritz.

As we live each day, I don't always feel sad. My frustration at looking for a missing sweater or hairbrush or cell phone,

Flat Iron Lake in winter

has changed to a game. I've become a sleuth in piecing together his footsteps and the trail I might have to follow to find something. The game is fun until he accuses me of hiding something from him. He loves it when I admit to forgetting a name or a fact. We joke about being in this together.

CNN aired a show this week entitled: *The Unthinkable: the Alzheimer's Epidemic.* Watching it together, I found myself wanting to shield Fritz from some of the stories of decline playing out before our eyes. He reacted to narrator Larry King's personality but not to the content of the show. Afterward I listened to his feelings. His overwhelming reaction: I don't want to go through this and I don't want you to have to go through this. He talked of taking risks—

perhaps to shorten his life. Go off into the woods and not return—riding his bike off into the sunset—stopping his many pills, cold turkey. Much of what he imagines, would require a thoughtful decision based on the circumstances. He cannot think of a time his memory loss will affect even those cognitive functions.

I tried to stay rational and reasoned, "When you get to the point where life is unacceptable for you, you may not have the capacity to choose a course. You can give us instructions for the 'what ifs' but neither you nor I will likely be able to do anything to shorten your life." Several times he said, "I believe the good Lord would understand." And so God will, but the law may not. He looks ahead and wants to avoid suffering for all of us. I look the same direction, wanting the same but ready to accept something quite different.

Last week we were among our most trusted friends—a group of guys and their wives from Muskegon who went to high school and college together. We have a tradition at our yearly dinner to give each couple a chance to tell of the happenings in their family. Before our turn came around, I asked Fritz, "Are you going to tell our friends?"

"Not yet; not while I am still pretty good." So we told about our sadness over our son's marriage and their responses were wonderfully supportive. I couldn't help thinking that if they knew the "bundle of troubles" facing us, they could better see our reality. Not yet—not while he still looks like an average seventy-three year old. We are not ready for a change in our relationships with friends. We are not ready for this sadness to spread to those we love, especially our age-mates who fear AZ more than cancer. We are not ready to let the word Alzheimer's be part of our conversation.

Maybe the Early Stage Support Group will help us share and prepare for the road ahead. As much as I hate the euphemisms: "really bad" and "losing it" there has to be some way to talk about Alzheimer's in a dignified way. I may not love the new vocabulary any better but I'll be forced to use it soon.

5/3/11

I'm _____, and I have dementia

Six weeks into our meetings of the Early Dementia Support Group, we welcomed a panel of experts on community resources. Before they began, the leader suggested that we introduce ourselves. Audrey started, "I'm Audrey, and they say I have dementia. This is my care partner, Henry." With a smile on his face, the man of the next couple said, "I'm Don and I have dementia. This is Barbara, my care partner." Then it was Fritz's turn and he followed suit. It may be the first time he has ever said the words, "I have dementia," and acknowledged me by my new title of care partner. Pat followed and introduced two of her adult children who were present. It could have been a meeting of Alcoholics Anonymous (AA).

Our group meets together for an hour and then splits into the "haves" and "have nots." After hearing the panel, our care partner's group talks about how far away it seems to each of us that we would need things like adult day care or respite care for that person who said so boldly in this non-threatening place, "I have dementia." Inwardly those same people say, "but I am not so bad or I'm not THAT bad!" In comparison to those in a later stage dementia, they are right.

We talked about our natural support groups of family, friends and co-workers—each thinking about how to increase those bonds now because they might be needed very soon.

Photographing wild flowers in Lead King Basin, Colorado

My mental wheels were turning. We could all see the need for our partner to experience success in "giving back" in some small ways. Audrey, a former teacher, was a good example. With the help of a young woman from a local senior center, she was able to read to young children in several schools.

At the seventh and final session, Barbara told the group how proud she was of Don because he went back to AA. My first thought was that his despair over dementia had driven him back to drink. Not so. Barbara knew he needed a support group; she knew how much, over the years, Don had depended on this local AA group to keep him sober. Then Don spoke up, "I figured that after twenty-three years of sobriety, I had something to offer, so I went back."

Tears came in response to his bravery. Returning to the people and place that once was his chief support to overcome addiction must have been as hard as it was hopeful. He was welcomed back warmly and his testimony encouraged strugglers of many sorts. But most of all he found a place where he could still give. He cannot conquer dementia like he once did alcohol but he can face it with his friends by his side.

Barbara is thankful for his renewed sense of purpose. Those regular meetings return structure to his life—something to get up for, people waiting to see him, and a message of hope.

I had to ask, "Don, did our introductions from last week, 'I am Don and I have dementia,' lead you and Barbara to think about returning to AA?" They grinned with satisfaction, "However it came about—it was good."

How can Fritz give back? Since retirement, he has been involved as a scientific trustee in meetings of a research institute as well as a member of the "visiting committee" at his former medical school. He is stepping away from those commitments because they are becoming stressful. It means a loss of identity for him.

He has his garden from which he will give away produce and advice freely about caring for plants to produce maximum vitality. He has created a beautiful space and welcomes others to enjoy the restored prairie and wildflowers. He gets help from his eldest granddaughter and, in turn, gives her his love of the earth and ways to be its keeper. He shares his material blessings faithfully. None of these "gifts" are new but he must know there are many ways he can give of himself after he puts his formal commitments aside.

Teacher, gardener, lover of the earth—his life is his legacy, which he freely gives.

6/19/11

Speaking at commencement

The nature photographer

My Support Group - A Motley Flock

"Birds of a feather flock together." A small flock is gathering among my circle of friends. People usually become friends because of shared interests, proximity or some emotional tie. My small flock is joined by a common challenge; the group is exclusive—we want to keep others out. We are women of about the same age, who are caught up in the disease of dementia—not our own but that of our husbands'.

Mary Jane, Marj, Barbara and I, hoping that another friend does not join us soon. Each is connected to me because of our common concern, by phone, email and an occasional meeting for lunch. The rest don't know each other, but together they have become a source of camaraderie and information for me that I freely share within the circle. Perhaps, as the disease progresses for each of our husbands, we will become a virtual small group.

I found Mary Jane during that awful time of seeing signs every day but not knowing what to do and where to go. To move ahead I needed to verify or rule out the signs and symptoms, but to do that I had to tell Fritz what I suspected. Neither I, nor our children, who had seen the same signs, knew how to talk about this with him. Mary Jane had been through all of that earlier when her husband was hospitalized because of a stroke-like attack, which lead to the diagnosis of dementia. My daughter put us in contact and we have depended on each other ever since. Both of our husbands are retired professors; both masked their losses for a long time because of high intelligence.

The story at the beginning of this collection, tells of Fritz meeting old friends while waiting to board the Milwaukee Clipper. That was Marj, a childhood classmate in Denver and her husband Curt. He is the cleverest man I know. He began as a house painter with an artistic flair and has been in great demand by the wealthy in Denver, not just to paint but to advise. Color, design, placement—Curt was a skilled interior decorator without the title. At home he built a model train with a whole village to house it, full of intricate detail. He loved to laugh at the tall tales of his own telling. He collected antiques and memorabilia from the Wild West days and converted part of their second floor into a "step back" into history. Seeing it was an amazing experience. Now, he can no longer hang a picture.

Barbara was part of the early dementia support group. I knew immediately that we should be friends. When we talked in the group without our husbands, I learned that Don has a daughter by a previous marriage who is in need of support by her father. Don is worried about providing for both his daughter and Barbara. She and I share concerns about our conflicting roles of being there for both our children and our partner.

The other person in the wings is a longtime friend but one I meet rarely. When I ask, "How's your husband?" she always says he is just fine. During our last long conversation, I got a hint that all was not well. Some of her concerns were like my own.

I need these women badly because I can't talk about dementia with other friends. More will join us—involuntarily but not invited. Each of our husbands will progress differently, but they will all go down an inevitable path. For me it was hard to see the difference between normal aging, and signs of mental decline. I have urged several friends to seek testing so at least they can utilize the drugs that are available to slow the progression. I'd like to save them from the dilemma of finding help.

Today, in an email posted at 5:30 in the morning, Mary Jane wrote: "Jim can no longer read." She didn't have to say more. I cried—for her, for Jim, for me, for Fritz—and everyone I know or can imagine who faces this awful disease. It drains away abilities and personality, leaving only the dregs.

I know in my head that God has promised never to leave us; in my heart I wonder where he is. Could it be that God is present through the women of our motley flock helping us stand together, wrapped in our mutual comforter? My hope is that with each other's support we can endure the dark days with the men we love and would never leave.

12/18/11

Pheasant hunting with Loran

When did I stop praying?

During next Sunday's worship service my turn comes to offer the "prayers of the people." I've always loved hearing and writing congregational prayers. As the date approached I thought about how different praying on behalf of a group is as opposed to saying a personal prayer. For a service, I have the advantage of having the morning liturgy in front of me: the songs, the prayers we speak together and the scriptural basis for the sermon. Sometimes I even know a bit of the content of the pastor's sermon. This week she will use Isaiah 43:2 — *When you pass through the waters, I will be with you; and through the rivers, they shall not overwhelm you; when you walk through fire you shall not be burned, and the flame shall not consume you.*

Garden in Winter

Writing the prayer becomes a creative experience of pulling many elements together to restate the message. In the light of everything that is happening right now, writing a prayer seems almost hypocritical. So often I cannot even pray my own prayers, so what am I doing uttering prayers for others?

My own prayers have no order or polish—they flow from whatever space my heart occupies. Maybe if I wrote down my own prayers, to myself, they would be coherent—but would they be honest? Are my feelings too raw to be written? I rush over the parts about praising or thanking God and get straight to the parts about my needs from God. Right now I am all need.

In former times when the turmoil in my life tried me to the breaking point, friends knew of my pain and assured me they were praying for me. This time is different. Not many of my friends know that my husband has been diagnosed with Alzheimer's. I know it is better not to say anything, yet those are exactly the friends who would pray when I cannot.

Only a few know that my son's marriage is breaking apart. Those who know, pray for him. At times like this I feel like no one can imagine how heavy the weight is on me. Trying to balance the needs between two men and not upset either father or son with bad news from the other, feels like dodging fire on both sides. Neither can help the other because of the burden of his own suffering. On my back their troubles are overwhelming. Like blazing fire and fast moving water, they have the power to consume me.

There are times, late at night, when I imagine myself in danger. Then my cries for help from God are spontaneous. I know God doesn't wait for me to inform him of how intolerable the present situation feels. The flames are coming closer; God must hear my cries.

My heart feels the deepest need to turn to God, but words and clear thoughts elude me. Weeks have passed without feeling his presence. Where is God?

Sunday comes. While listening to the pastor's sermon, I realize that my prayer glosses over the rest of the text: "I have called you by name; you are mine." Is God calling my name? I can't hear it but have to believe that God is trying to find me—to rescue me.

Stepping onto the pulpit and unfolding the paper prayer, my eyes sweep over a sea of faces. Who out there is hurting?

So many. Their concerns differ from my own, but many come with a burden. Maybe some also find it impossible to pray but seek out this place of communal prayer. At the end of my prayer, without script, I add: "Be with all of us who feel as though we, at times, are being tried by fire. We ask for tangible evidence of your promise—one that shows us you will not let the fire consume us."

I can no longer hide behind the editorial "we." Alone, I am searching for God to make good on those promises: alone, I am listening for God's voice, calling my name. One day will it be heard? My burdens must get lighter—let it be soon. I want to pray again.

5/15/11

CHAPTER FOUR

SEEING THE DISEASE CLEARLY

Recycling and Memory

Today Fritz announced that he had driven to the recycle center with our cardboard boxes. I looked around and immediately realized he had not taken the bulging bag of bottles and cans or the papers. "Why didn't you…?" slipped out of my mouth before I could check myself. "You never told me," was his answer. Lately I must answer multiple questions about where to dispose of all types of things. Where does this go? Which one is trash? Only now has it become a problem. In my mind, I review step-by-step all the details in order to understand his confusion about what goes where. It may explain other lapses.

We try to be ecologically conscious out here in the country. We compost in a bin a distance from the house and recycle everything we can. I dutifully save all my Diet Coke bottles and give them to a grandson to redeem for gas money because I hate putting them, one-by-one, into the return slots. We conserve electricity, purchase the eco-friendly bulbs, and use geothermal heating and cooling. Some would not have the patience to save, crush and sort all the refuse, but I can't help myself. I grew up in an era when tossing so much as a gum wrapper on the ground was slothful. I can't exactly hear my mother's voice in my head—but I'm sure she is behind most of my frugality and care of trash.

There are four ways to handle stuff in the house that we can no longer use: vegetable scraps and fruit skins go under the sink in a covered pail; trash goes in the plastic bag lined pullout drawer bin; cans and bottles in the bin directly behind in same pullout; paper and crushed cartons go into a bag in the closet. When the inside bins, bags and pails are full they need to graduate to the next step. The compost pail needs to be emptied into the compost bin out by the corner of the garden and stirred around with an auger-like tool. When the trash bag is full, it goes out into a larger plastic lined bin in the garage. Once a week we have to bring that plastic bag of trash to the end of our long driveway and deposit it into a roller bin for roadside pick up. The same overflow system is true for recyclable paper and cans and bottles, from which I sort out the returnables. Every few months, I deliver the recycle bottles, cans, paper and flattened corrugated boxes to the Kent County Recycle Center about twenty minutes away. Now that I write this out, I see how confusing it could be; I can unpack this complex process only because of memory.

Something else that requires memory is a story. For a while, Fritz has had trouble finding and using the identifying word when trying to relate a particular story. He can be well into the tale before I understand the basics: who, what, when and where. The middle often comes before the beginning. Fortunately, many of his stories are ones I have heard before. I've become a detective in catching a clue and building a whole framework within which the story makes sense. The problem intensifies when he is telling the story to someone else. I really need to be present to slip in a word now and then or the listener would be totally lost.

In the past I had speculated about word finding as a memory matter. No amount of filling in the word for him has lead to finding it the next time. The same is true when recalling the names for our different kinds of "refuse" and the proper place to put it. As I've been told in caregiver classes, all these behaviors are tied to memory. The same is true for any organizing, task planning, making judgments—they all require short-term memory.

Simplify the task, the teachers say, so he will experience success. I don't know how to do that with the recycle routine, but I have tried that with his computer. He was never a whiz at word processing because he had a secretary all of his working life. But he gained competence early in retirement, even going so far as to make his own labels for each file folder. About five years ago we changed from a PC to a Mac and he had to learn a different system. At first he seemed to latch onto the differences but now he is losing even those skills. He only uses the computer for email, storing pictures and occasionally clicking on a link to the Internet. His plaintive calls have become more frequent: "I wrote a whole letter and I think I lost it." "How do I find a letter that I got yesterday?" "Nothing comes up when I hit _____."

We have a little Radio Shack intercom connecting my desk on the second floor with his on the lower level. In the past I'd try to address the problem remotely—now I just race down the two flights of stairs to solve it. I used to try to teach while in the process of fixing but he tells me he will not remember the next time. He suggests I make lists of steps or diagrams and I try, only to realize that he cannot locate the aids when he needs them, much less follow the steps. He does not dare to send an email until I review it. "I hate to call you all the time," he says with tears in his eyes. The whole situation unnerves him.

I am saddened every day; I understand how much he has lost. Every Thursday when the trash has to be brought out to the road, he asks, "Which bag?" Even as I answer, the pain shows on his face. Simple things are slipping away; he is at first surprised and then horribly discouraged. These are not temporary losses; once a skill is gone, it is not coming back.

Despite his losses he is left with lifelong instincts to "get something done" or accomplish things every day—desire for satisfaction of a job well done is strong. His oderly side still shows itself in his beloved garden and his clean garage. Again, I am often the key to this kind of closure around a task that has to be done a certain way. I've learned to pick up that broom or hoe and ask what more he wants me to do.

Even considering all he has lost, I pray that we find pleasant days and abundant summer gardens for many years. He may not be able to say the names of the plants or the vegetables but he knows how to make them grow, beautiful and delicious. Cleaning away garage dirt requires no memory. The shine of a clean garage makes him smile. Clean cars in a clean garage satisfy his longing for order. For now, his pleasure in seeing the neat rows of healthy plants overcomes the pain of a dying memory.

Whatever the challenge, he and I will move on together— one season at a time.

6/6/11

5th grade b-ball team

Nostalgia—Long-term Memory Embellished

Coming home from Lake Michigan on highway U.S. 31, Fritz announces that he wants to take a quick ride through his hometown, Muskegon. We have nothing on the schedule so why not? Entering Muskegon on Seaway Drive, he wants to go down a street called Getty which has two long dips before leading up to the street of his youth, Oak. At the low point, just before the rise, he remembers when the rich bottomland was filled with celery in season. A creek (pronounced "crick" in these parts) that ran through the fields was accessible from his house "up the hill." This field represents the scene of his childhood—a place of wonder for a nature-loving boy.

We drive slowly down Oak Street as he recalls the neighbors by their houses, even though some of the structures have fallen to disrepair. When the white bungalow comes in view, we can see the same hanging wooden "604" sign over the front door that his dad had made and placed there more than seventy years earlier. The exterior of the house looks sound, still painted white with green trim. The driveway remains unpaved but neighbor Albert Bosch's little shack next door has long since been razed. The garage with its square of concrete, the scene of many a basketball contest between the four brothers, is hidden behind a fence.

The house's front door stands open on this warm summer day, so Fritz knocks on the frame. He hopes to get permission to walk to the back of the narrow lot and see the hill where he spent endless hours and the creek where he fished. I stay in the car until he comes back to get his camera. For some reason the man asks him to walk on the left side of the house. We wander back together.

We walk past his mom's long abandoned flowerbed, the tall fence surrounding the garage and an adjacent baseball lot on the left—to the small open strip before the "back hill." Fritz delights that his mom's snowball tree is still there; I share memories with him of the big Mulberry tree that used to drop berries on the lawn chairs. The location of his dad's vegetable garden and tool shed is not visible, now encased within the fence, sharing space with an old travel trailer.

We are satisfied with just a glimpse. Fritz raises his camera to record the demise of this beloved place he called home. Suddenly doors open on the backsides of the surrounding houses bordering the empty lot and several people move toward us. A particularly menacing man with a scruffy beard and large belly comes out of the back door of Fritz's old house. We try to make conversation. Fritz recalls his mom's garden and the trumpet vine that brightened the backside of the house. He asks the burly, uninterested man if he ever tried fishing in the creek. His look is of the "you've got to be kidding" kind. "That was then; this is now," he says. "You liven' in the past, I live in the present and the future."

We say our thanks, hurry to the car and drive off—the closest we have ever come to being run off the land. Fritz and I think back to after his mother died when his nephew owned the house briefly, he converted the tiny house into three single apartments. Most likely the front door man has no contact with the back door man and neither know the person upstairs. The house has become just one more marginal rental in the core city.

Interestingly, Fritz is not fazed by our non-welcome but talks all the way home about the olden days when the white frame house was home and his neighborhood beautiful. I think of his humble beginnings and how his parents made this place seem like a castle because of their love of home and family.

The new tenant is right; Fritz is living in the past. Today it is a blessed place to live; those good old days are better for Fritz than the ones he is living right now. Near memory may be fleeting but long-term memory is today's precious gift.

6/9/11

A Crazy Summer

By summer our family had adapted to Fritz's limitations and planned our annual cross-country trip to Colorado. Our destination, as always, was the little town of Marble, in the Crystal River Valley. My parents found and bought an old clapboard house in the deserted quarrying town in the early 50s and I, and my extended family, have come every year since. There was no other place we'd rather be. After Doug's accident, we built a cabin up the hill that had fewer barriers. Between the two houses there was plenty of sleeping space.

The rest of the family, including a cousin, drove but we decided to fly because we wanted to stay an extra week. Already the year before, I noticed that the noise and confusion of so many people bothered Fritz. An extra week by ourselves sounded good.

We flew to Denver and rented a car but kept in touch with the other three cars that were to pass through Denver about the same time. After getting through the city and beginning the assent past Red Rocks and up the foothills our spirits rose too. The first sight over the ridge was always breathtaking when we found ourselves in the mountains, surrounded often by snow-covered peaks. But just at the pinnacle we got an urgent call from Idaho Springs saying that one of the cars had lost its brakes. Unbelievably, on the steep mountain highway, the driver had been able to bring it to a stop. The near tragedy left everyone stunned.

Fortunately we had not yet passed the town and could stop and help decide what to do. They were already searching for a repair option in this small mountain town. The work couldn't be done right away so we consolidated baggage and people in ours and the other two cars and continued four more hours to Marble. We always stop for supplies at the last town because there are no grocery stores where we are going. Our biggest problem was to find room for food in the already stuffed vehicles.

Talking photography with grandson Matt

That was enough excitement for one day and I hoped the rest of the week would be calm, at least as calm as a group of seventeen would be. The grandkids pair up closely by ages so they made their own fun. We kept an old jeep up there because Marble was at the end of the road for all but four-wheel drive vehicles. Fritz was physically fit and ready to walk and climb and fish for trout. Everyone was active and always hungry.

With that many people, meals were a big production. The old house has the bigger table so we ate all our main meals there. Only a few days into the week, as Fritz was walking with some of the group down the hill from the cabin to the house for supper he suddenly noticed his tongue was swelling. One

Eating lunch beside the old Jeep

side of his tongue was about three times its size. Our son-in-law, Steve, a doctor, immediately saw the potential danger of swelling and restricted breathing. He always carries some emergency meds so gave him something and then rushed with us to the nearest hospital emergency room over an hour away.

During the next hours we speculated over anything that could have brought on the swelling, while the ER doctor gave medications to reverse it. Fritz was only released with meds and an epinephrine pen because we had a doctor with us. We watched warily for two days, hoping it would pass. But then in the middle of the night Fritz felt the swelling again but this time on the opposite side of his tongue. Steve was in the other house so Fritz and I threw on some clothes and went there to wake him up. The swelling was not as severe but worried us all night. In the morning we changed our return flight and went home early. Fritz needed a complete medical work-up to get to the bottom of the cause.

Everyone was baffled. We kept the emergency supplies ready but there was no more swelling. Our questions were not answered but both of us felt more than a little cheated out of our summer vacation.

He Brought Me Roses

Sunday morning dawned bringing me a vague sense of loneliness. The house was quiet; the dog and Fritz still sleeping. My usual morning ritual of reading the news online over my first cup of tea seemed all too commonplace for this day in late August, the day of my birth. There was a time when my children forced me to stay in bed until they delivered a birthday breakfast. Many birthdays were spent at a Lake Michigan cottage, savoring the last week of our summer vacation before teaching and school began. The chaotic crowds of summer's past have given way to just the two of us, keeping company throughout predictable days. Birthdays, holidays, special occasions so easily meld into average, unmarked days.

On my birthday, I expected no more. Long before his diagnosis, Fritz was not a birthday keeper. He let the kids make their fuss over me and he joined in. When our family nest emptied over twenty-five years ago, so did celebrations other than our casual greetings of "Happy Birthday." Some years ago he, along with every member of the family, forgot my sixtieth birthday—the one that prompted me to write an essay I called, "Birthday Blues."

But once he remembered or I broke the birthday news, he was happy to take me out for dinner. If he could not find the card he tucked into the back of his desk drawer purchased soon after his own birthday so he wouldn't forget, he made an excuse and went shopping.

He always spent a long time selecting just the right sentiment from the greeting card rack. If I ever wondered what his mysterious foray to the store was on my day—it would be for the mushy, love card—saying the things he could not quite put into words. Sometimes he even brought roses.

Today will probably be no different. Part of his dementia shows in a preoccupation with himself. Each day I get a litany of his ills—sometimes more than once. His ailments, real and imagined, press upon him with something like tunnel vision. I am the only one within earshot so he asks my advice on everything from bleeding cuts to trouble swallowing. I try to listen but my advice seems worthless (even to me) and goes unheeded.

This August 28 the news about the approaching Hurricane Irene will divert our attention for a while. Soon my cup of tea is gone and I go out to walk the dog. The morning is already muggy so after feeding Jake I head straight toward the shower, passing the room where I recently sat. A flash of deep red catches my eye. There next to my laptop is a vase containing a dozen long-stemmed red roses and the sure-to-be sentimental card next to it.

He hears my gasp. Fritz stands lurking in the doorway, still in his pajamas, waiting to enjoy his surprise. He comes out looking disheveled with his silver gray bed-hair, but is soon grinning with glee. I hug him—full of thanks. How extraordinary that during this year of forgetfulness, he remembers the thing that always means so much to me—a little fuss on my birthday. At this moment, I love him more than ever.

Later I ask if one of the kids had reminded him. He denies it but I soon learned that the afternoon before our daughter had asked him to hand deliver the card she didn't get mailed on time. The trip from her home to ours takes about thirty minutes but it took him an hour and a half to get home after he searched for flowers. Much later I realized that he had driven way out of his way, all the way across town, to get the flowers—to the only place he could remember had them.

He brought me roses!

9/2/11

And The Good News Is: It is NOT Alzheimer's

In the new session of "Writing Memoir" which I teach at Calvin College's Academy for Lifelong Learning, a man who I will call Jim seemed confused by the assignment at the first class. "Memories rely on triggers," I suggested, "so let's think about one of our senses—touch—and see what comes to mind." I passed around several objects that quickly became known, not because of their visual qualities, but by touch. We thought of more instances of "touch" and put them on one of two lists: hate or love. Jim admitted confusion when it came to letting touch trigger a memory. "Think of the touch of someone's hand," I said. A few minutes later I noticed he had his head down almost as if he had fallen asleep. I thought he might not come back to the next class.

When I asked the organizer of the program about him, she said, "Did you know his wife was recently diagnosed with

Alzheimer's?" Of course I did not, but it made me want to reach out to him because of the diagnosis our spouses shared.

Before the second class I saw Jim in the campus coffee shop and struck up a conversation with, "I understand we have something in common." He looked puzzled at first until I said one word "dementia." He opened up immediately and we talked about his nearly three-year awakening to his wife's condition and his altered life. He described several incidents of losing her, one of which happened recently on this campus when they took a course together. He turned around and she was gone. After a futile search in the logical places they alerted the campus police, who found her because of a tip from an observant student. Each time she wandered, she was spared harm until one day she fell while straying in their large backyard—and broke her hand.

As we pieced together our similar but unique journeys, I asked when he first knew. He talked of tests and scans and finally the doctor's diagnosis. "Some kind of dementia…" he said, "but the good news is that it is NOT Alzheimer's." I swallowed hard and said lamely, "I guess it doesn't matter what name you give it—the effects are the same.

I have another friend whose husband exhibits behaviors similar to my husband's. They, too, were reassured it was not Alzheimer's, because it came on so gradually. They lived in a state of denial for years as he began the familiar downward path.

So much for semantics. I try to understand why dodging the Alzheimer's word may feel good for a while. Finally, in our case, it was a relief to call these strange behaviors by a name. Often, before you tell a friend what you know, the friend already has a clue. "Uncharacteristic, odd, surprising" are words used to describe the behavior of the person they thought they knew well.

What is the sensory impact of hearing or seeing the word Alzheimer's in print? The word is laden with baggage of fear, dread, and vivid examples of people you once knew who were gradually lost to this disease. Dementia might sound softer and more soothing—an easier way to break the news. But avoiding the label's reality lasts only so long. There are many forms and iterations of dementia and progression varies, but the direction is only one way.

The farther my friends and I go as "care partners" the more we realize that labels mean nothing. We can share our hopes, our frustrations, our sadness and even hints for coping but we cannot shed the mantle we have inherited. We love a person deeply and he or she needs us now like never before.

My reference to the sense of "touch" brought on a physical reaction in Jim. Perhaps his wife's touch was becoming impersonal with dementia, as he experienced little or no response to his care. I long to preserve the "loving touch" with hugs each morning or after we have been apart. We sometimes hold hands while watching TV or I rub his back in bed. We always kiss goodnight. I pray that he never loses the comfort of my touch and I never lose the assurance of his love, as our hands or lips meet. Touch may someday transcend other forms of communication, as words and thoughts slip away.

9/24/11

Winter stalks

The Tale of Stalks

A mild day greets me on my walk out of the garage and onto the wet pavement. In mid-November the air feels crisp with its gentle scents. The overcast sky lets through only diffuse light. If it were a good day for pictures I would record the defoliated scene of our front yard and rain garden. The chest high stalks met the weed-whacker yesterday when the stiff goldenrod looked more like weeds than flowers, tops bending haphazardly with their fuzzy heads going to seed.

Over the years we have debated about clearing the stalks in fall or spring. The alternative to cutting them now is to let them flatten with the weight of snow and pick up the dead stalks in spring when the days get warmer. Both plans require lots of work, but recently the clean-cut look close to the house appeals to us. Beyond our yard, we are surrounded by the natural growth and slight stoop of the prairie grasses because of their hearty summer growth. Soon snow will weigh down those stalks in picturesque mounds.

While most people rake leaves, Fritz and I rake stalks, pile them on the little cart behind the golf cart and dump them among the trees along the lake. He always initiates the work while I pretend that winter is not just around the bend. I resist hard physical work in favor of more heady stuff. Finally, we have no choice but to work together and get the job done. He is fussy about his work and my job must match his vision. My "good enough" is never good enough for him.

We work side by side, both tiring more quickly than when we were young. I push myself to stay on-task long after my shoulders ache and my back complains. He looks terribly tired but will rarely give himself permission to take a break. As with so many other outdoor chores he puts his hands to, he sees a weather deadline looming. This forces us to complete the task now, not tomorrow when we have regained our strength. "It is supposed to rain tomorrow. If we don't finish, we are doomed." I am much more measured about the disaster that awaits but can never convince him.

What I see after this warm morning is the neat and complete look of a job well done. I cannot call it pretty any more than the aftermath of our annual spring burn. After the fire, the green signs of new growth soon give assurance that dormant life is waking up. In November, that month I find so hard to love, the clean-cut look of the yard just looks like death. The end of things is never as glorious as their beginning.

During the fall as I watch Fritz taking care of things outside and inside the house, I know I should be taking notes. We are traditional in many ways—long ago we divided tasks and took care of the things we knew most about. Occasionally we ask the other for help with "our work" but each of us concentrates on those things we have always done. The feminist in me sees a beautiful balance in our shared leadership. The realist I have become, sees the balance shifting with all the tasks slowly rolling toward me. I am totally unprepared. The sewer, the heating/cooling system, the eaves, the driveway, the barn full of machines—each with its own fuel container—I will never be able to keep them straight.

We had an incident this fall with the furnace. Fritz wanted to make sure the humidifier was on because air in the house felt too dry. He fussed with the controls and looked downstairs at the unit before deciding that the humidifier only goes on when the furnace is turned to cooling. I objected from my limited knowledge saying it did not make sense. He insisted and soon the air conditioning was running full blast—on a cold, forty-degree day. Only then did he concede he had it wrong. Better add that to my list.

A circuit breaker blew while I was away and he did not remember how to find and throw the breaker back on. Add that to the list. I have never driven the mower or the tractor or run the weed-whacker. Should I ask him to teach me now while he still can? Even if he could, he would detect my fake interest.

I decided last year after his diagnosis of dementia that I would not try to anticipate trouble but live in the present. Why think of the "might be's" when the present transitions are hard enough? As I walk around the drive and see the fruits of our work I can't help thinking what else should be on the list.

The act of taking care of the dead stalks suggests that it is already too late to have a smooth transition into his jobs. He has always done them one way. I should have learned by watching because now it is too late for explanations. Like a relay runner, I just have to grab the baton and run.

Those stalks were not cut down in their prime—it was their time. Their seeds continued to scatter even while we carried them away. Surely wild goldenrod will come back tenfold.

We are no longer in our prime. How will we return next spring? Will both of us be able to ask for help to accomplish our work? Will we still bloom?

11/14/11

Didn't you just say that?

Anyone who has given me a paper to edit or has turned in a memoir essay in the classes I teach can tell you what I dislike the most. I have built-in radar that hones in on one particular trouble spot—repeated words. My father used to have a similar distain for mispronounced words—they seemed to rub him the wrong way and he was not reluctant to tell me. I try to be kind, but when I have seen a word or phrase before in a piece, I mark it with a big RED, for redundant.

When reading, my ears hear the words from the page. I just don't like to hear the same thing twice. It shocks my ear like butchered words upset my dad. Perhaps I am looking for creativity of expression; a repeat suggests to me that the writer is using a lot of fall-back words and phrases. I understand because I can neither see nor hear my own.

Listening to national news during supper, one on NBC and then one on public television, I get saturated with repeated stories, not verbatim but with all the facts the same, taken from the same wire service. My husband likes the repeat; it helps him remember. The other night I heard the same clever, ear-catching commercial three times in a row and went ballistic before I could find the mute button.

When Fritz repeats something he has told me before, my hackles go up. My average memory has logged that information—I don't need another layer of the same. His faltering memory has no recall of saying that before. Back when I assumed he just was not paying attention, I would say, not so gently, "You told me that before!" Over time, I realized that he really didn't remember and I tried to hold my tongue. But it was hard. The redundancy radar just would not turn off.

When I attended a caregiver's class, I heard what I already knew: scolding about repeats is the worst thing you can do. It emphasizes to the person you love that they are failing. It does not help them to be criticized for something over which they have no control. It won't encourage them to try harder. Out of fear they may stop telling you things altogether. As hard as it is to fathom the wound of a simple retort, if not checked, may be the beginning of elder abuse.

Careful listener that I am, I have had to turn off the instinct to note all things repeated. Perhaps it will help me not to react to other aversions, like commercials I've heard umpteen times or Christmas "musak" in all the stores this time of year. I have long been bothered by hearing Fritz telling the same stories to the grandchildren, until I read a quote by Groucho Marx: "If you've heard this story before, don't stop me, because I'd like to hear it again."

In Uganda

But there is more to this story. My aversion to repeating makes me doubly conscious of what I have said and when I have said it. It may be like an internal ticker tape to keep me from repeating myself. When I am accused of not telling Fritz something—I rebel. I did, but he can't remember it. Now I really want to defend myself when he says, "You never told me that." Or even more difficult to handle, the accusation, "Why didn't you tell me that?" I never thought that his loss of short-term memory could impact me so heavily.

I've tried strategies like going over each day's plans first thing in the morning or writing them on sticky notes for the refrigerator. He keeps a calendar—but does not look at it, and is often surprised when I tell him of an appointment we made long ago. It is not only his schedule he forgets but mine too. I have gone to our son's house almost every Thursday for the last few years. But even when I remind him in the morning, as I pack up to go he says, "where are you going?" Multiple plans are really difficult to remember, so I tell him my main destination and the generic "errands." He always wants to know when I am coming back. Because we live about forty minutes north of town, it is difficult to estimate when, exactly, I'll be home. Occasionally on my return, he is irritated because he thought I would be home much earlier.

In the same way that repeated words or phrases do nothing to help an essay or a letter, my repeating does not help him. His own repetition of questions or comments does not irritate him, only his closest listener—me. His not-knowing what he said before, shields him from constant embarrassment—a perverse benefit of his loss. Otherwise it would be devastating.

Think of all the things you do every day that rely on your memory. Even the most disorganized among us remember that a certain bill passed through our hands, even if we cannot put our finger on it immediately. To look for something lost, we have to remember that it is missing. Often he only knows it is missing when we review: wallet, keys, cell phone, hearing-aids. The search begins: pant pockets, jacket pockets, bathroom, bed stand, closet, desk. But, just to keep me humble, the other day I found a long-lost second key to the car in my own briefcase. On days like that my fear increases: could dementia be happening to me?

Fritz had a painful test recently. On the way home he tried to describe it to me: "just like when you were a kid and someone pulled your arm backward behind your back." As

I was pondering how that might feel, because it had never happened to me, he repeated it again—two times within about five minutes. I'm thankful he is still talking to me; repeated words are better than no words at all.

I'll train my ear to accept his repeats. That does not mean I will embrace the redundancy of others or myself with any more pleasure. The instinct is strong: get rid of repeated words and phrases whenever possible. But when I cannot, just accept it as one more story that he just likes to hear again.

12/3/11

Telling the Stories of Others

I made a vow last month: to write my husband's stories. I didn't just speak it, I wrote it in an essay and read it to my writing group. That almost makes it a legal document.

On Thanksgiving Day after the crowd was gone and the seldom-used serving dishes washed and stowed, I remembered the vow. The day with its non-stop activity left Fritz exhausted, but pleased that everyone was here. "This was a good day," he remarked from his easy chair. "What do you remember of past Thanksgivings?" I asked, trying to prime the memory pump. "When you were young, how did you celebrate? What kinds of things did your mom cook?"

He did not say much but my own memory of Thanksgivings with his family lit up. I may have attended the last holiday meal of his mom's extended family, in the "fire-barn" in Whitehall with a decidedly older crowd. I recall that people sat on folding chairs along the wall and no one spoke to me. Food was abundant—conversation sparse. Shocking to me that people who knew each other well had so little

In Kenya

to say and so little curiosity about a newcomer like me. My own Thanksgiving memories were of many people, mostly strangers, becoming friends over turkey and gravy eaten around a cloth covered ping-pong table in our basement. Mom liked a crowd but we had no family in Denver, so she searched "the highways and byways," to fill the table.

After a few minutes of Fritz's short answers to my questions about Thanksgiving's past, I stopped probing. It wasn't the time or the topic to spur his memory of stories past.

One morning, a few days later, Fritz suddenly appeared in my study. After telling me earlier how tired he was before retreating to his basement office, I was very surprised to see him. That he climbed two flights of stairs when he could have used the intercom—made me curious. He had been reading some science or health related material and came across one about non-Hodgkin's Lymphoma. At first I wondered if he was convinced he had the disease. Not at all—he came to talk about his most noteworthy discovery during a career in biochemistry. His basic science work was an important factor leading to the drug, Rituxan, which effectively combats that type of cancer.

His excitement grew as he retold parts of a story that I knew well. It went from the serendipity of his first discoveries to the equally strange story of how his "3-prime cap structure" was patented, against his advice, by Upjohn Pharmaceuticals. "I worked on this problem because it was fascinating to me, not because I could imagine anything practical coming from it," he confessed. The Upjohn patent of his work went ahead and twenty years later it was found to aid in drug production.

We went on to talk about basic science. Years of persistence and patience are required just to understand a tiny part of how the body works at the molecular level. Bench science, that not-so-glamorous preoccupation with the microbial world, is far removed from the practice of medicine that will someday dispense its benefits. Those who deliver the breakthrough treatments are very seldom the ones that discover them. They may have been involved in clinical trials, which are very important for drug approval, but not the beginning of the raw materials or building blocks that are so vital to the process.

"That's the story of my whole career," he said. "Opportunities came that I never expected and I certainly never deserved." He was animated while talking—all tiredness gone. His eyes lit up as if they were seeing puzzles in basic science that he might still want to tackle. He was not in a hurry to leave.

Suddenly I realized that this was the moment I had tried to prime. He was remembering the things that were important to him—things worth sharing. And then he said it: "This story should be told." Suddenly this story, among the many happenings in his life, became so important that he forgot all else to come and talk about it.

Fritz knew nothing about my vow. Talk about serendipity!

And there is more. That day I had read a part in Dan Taylor's book, *Creating a Spiritual Legacy,* —about writing stories for people who find it difficult. For many years, Fritz has expressed a desire to tell his stories. We even went to a condo in Florida for a week one winter and set out to do just that. He made lots of notes, but wrote no stories. He thinks about that desire from time to time but can't bring himself to do it. His excuses are classic: if only he could learn to use the voice dictation system on his computer again; if only he had a tape-recorder (he does) to dictate his stories; and, if only he could find the time. But he, like so many people, is a storyteller, not a storywriter. His stories come spontaneously in conversation, often with his grandchildren.

The longest sample story in Dan Taylor's book is his own story about his mother. He used it ostensibly to show many things about writing stories. The story may have centered on his mother, but he was a character as he related scenes from their interactions in a dementia care center. He decided what to tell and what to show. It was his story about her story, the present situation augmented by snippets of her past. Now I was hooked. My present preoccupation is gleaning my husband's stories before dementia silences them. At one time Fritz didn't know where to start and how to write the stories that mattered to him. Now he cannot. Clearly, when he mounts the stairs to tell me about something in his life, I must be his storywriter. The results will always be his story colored by my words but that is better than no stories.

To reiterate Frederick Buechner's words; "To lose track of our stories is to be profoundly impoverished not only humanly but also spiritually." I cannot let his legacy be lost; I must tell his stories through our shared story. I won't have to do much research of all the years we have been together, as long as my memory holds. For that reason alone, I have to start today.

12/4/11

More Mysteries

Soon after our day of hard labor, Fritz began complaining of a dull pain in his cheek. The tongue-swelling incident may have made him even more conscious of changes around his mouth and neck. To show me he would put his palm on his face as you might do when thinking about something. I didn't react immediately to his vague description and he tried hard to forget it. Fritz has always been hyper-aware of changes in his body. Unlike some men, he does not hesitate to get professional advice.

Finally when the pain didn't go away, he decided to make an appointment. He and his internist thought it might have something to do with the tongue swelling but could make no connection. Fritz already had an appointment with an ear, nose and throat specialist about the cause of the tongue enlargement so while there, he mentioned almost offhand, about the sensation in his cheek. The doctor probed and with Fritz's help could pinpoint the place where it hurt.

The doctor ordered scans to get a view inside. He saw a small mass, which was then biopsied. The report came back positive for cancer on the salivary gland. When the doctor called soon after Thanksgiving, he had more bad news. There was another tumor on the other side of his jaw. Soon we found that the second one was not cancerous, but the doctor felt it was urgent that both be removed without delay. Surgery was scheduled for mid-December. The question came up about removing both tumors at the same time. Even though one surgery might last up to five hours, it seemed a better option than two operations and two hospitalizations.

I sat in the hospital family waiting room while Fritz was in surgery. In comparison to other surgeries this one felt minor. However, I remembered the post-surgery period of confusion after Fritz's transplant and began to worry about anesthesia and dementia. Would it be worse this time? He was physically stronger now but mentally weaker. We are in new territory.

The surgery was a little shorter than anticipated and the doctor brought a good report. Later in the hospital room, Fritz didn't have much pain but he seemed baffled by all the attention and questions. Minus his hearing aids, he couldn't understand the multitude of questions delivered by several providers. He seemed to be in a fog. Soon it was clear that he could not be left alone in the hospital overnight. I honestly never considered that he would need one of us there. Barb must have seen my fatigue and offered to spend the night.

Christmas followed much too soon. The family gathered but Fritz sat quietly on his chair and was not fully engaged. We looked ahead to the New Year with heavy hearts. Why do all these odd things always happen to Fritz? Considering the weight of dementia, fairness would have spread the pain away from him and toward me. Enough is enough! I longed for speedy recovery and better health for the New Year.

It is routine after the removal of a cancerous tumor to have a consultation with an oncologist. Even though the surgeon was certain he had removed all the affected tissue and Fritz would not need radiation, we went for the consult. When the doctor told us he would recommend six weeks of daily radiation, Fritz turned to him saying, "I am seventy-four and have Alzheimer's. What is the point?" The physician was unmoved. He said because the type of cancer was "undifferentiated," he had to stand by his judgment.

Before going on summer vacation, we had toyed with the idea of going back to Africa since last January's trip had gone quite well. But after both of these incidents it was clear he would be recuperating, starting treatment and we would not be going anywhere. We ended the year much as it had begun with lowered expectations for the future.

12/30/11

Fritz beside compass plant at Flat Iron Lake

CHAPTER FIVE

READING THE FORECAST: STORM CLOUDS

Question Time – Where is God in all of this?

The new list for Sunday night covenant groups is tucked into the church bulletin today. Despite the fact that we probably will not be joining any study groups this season, Fritz and I read them eagerly. So many interesting topics: *Christians and the 2012 Presidential Election; Understanding our Neighbors; Sing a new Song; and Justification* (i.e by faith). But the one we both gravitate to is *Dementia and the Christian Community*. On the way home, Fritz muses, "I wonder if I should offer to go?" I am surprised he would think of such a public forum.

Covenant groups are a way for our congregation to "repurpose" the archaic evening worship service with something more relevant. The concept of study groups evolved over time to include about a dozen adult groups meeting simultaneously, along with the youth groups that formerly met during the week. Although it makes for a busy Sunday every other week, it brings families together to a place where there is something for everyone. The evening begins with a kid-friendly service with lots of musical participation by young adults and audio-visual enhancement. Afterward we share a simple meal before the groups begin.

My surprise at Fritz's remark came because most of the people at our church do not know that he has a diagnosis of dementia. We have taken the advice of our Alzheimer's support group and operate on a need-to-know basis. However, when close friends are told, some have admitted to me that they suspected something was amiss. A year ago, at another covenant group centering on a science topic, Fritz realized that he could not be the resource the leader hoped for even though he had spent his entire working life in biological sciences. He could no longer find the words to explain what he once knew. He stopped going out of fear that more questions would come his way.

We both know that dementia is nothing to be ashamed of. It is not a disease one can prevent by living a healthy lifestyle. Fritz loved reading a collection of articles in a publication called *Mind, Mood and Memory* and would have done anything to preserve his memory. He faithfully underlined all relevant information and researched some further. We have always eaten a healthy diet full of vegetables and fruit, exercised regularly and read widely. The likely causes are as genetic as inheriting his father's kidney disease. His mother suffered from dementia later in her life.

What would he say to the group who set out to ponder the stated questions: how do we relate to those with dementia or Alzheimer's in our family and church communities? How do we support caregivers? What is the role of the church? Where is God in all of this? I asked Fritz these questions and he quickly strayed from them to thoughts of his own.

For my part I have just begun to grapple with the very questions raised. One leader is a woman whose father has dementia; she is about the same age as our children. The caregiver's class that I took stressed circles of support, the family being the first. I know our kids would do anything for their dad and me. But they are sandwiched between ongoing demands of their own maturing children and their once very self-sufficient parents. Would I ever ask one of them to spend the day with Fritz allowing me to hole up in my study and write? Never. Would I ask one of them to drive him to appointments when I am perfectly able? Probably not. If someone from the church would offer, I would probably count their cost above my own. Will all those things take a toll on me? Yes.

Back to those questions for the church community.

When someone is known to have a chronic illness, mental or physical, the tendency is for others to see the disease before everything else. I do it myself. Out of care we inquire about their wellbeing. The person and his/her partner become objects of pity. But pity is what many will never get beyond. It has happened with my son. Some acquaintances just can't get beyond the wheelchair he uses to see the real guy who sits there.

And then the 64,000 dollar question—where does God come into all this? In an email from a friend whose husband also has dementia, came the question: "Oh, how much more can the Lord lay upon us?" I would never look at it that way but this illness still shakes my faith. The other day, Fritz and I were discussing how President Obama is blamed for all that goes wrong—but never praised when something goes right. Perhaps the opposite is true here—we praise God for all the blessings but dare not curse God for all the trials. "Praise God from whom all blessings flow…" never gets to what you do about the rest. Blame? Rant about fairness? Think fatalistically…whatever will be will be?

My sister gave me a book about a theology of suffering by Richard Rohr, the same Franciscan priest who wrote, *Falling Upward*. He says, "Sooner or later, if you are on any classic 'spiritual schedule,' some event, person, death, idea or relationship will enter your life that you simply cannot deal with, using your present skill set, your acquired knowledge or your strong willpower. Spiritually speaking, you will be, you must be, led to the edge of your own private resources." At that point you hit the stumbling stone, says Rohr. Then it does not matter where the suffering came from, you only know you cannot get through it alone. And there you find God—not as you imagined God to be, all-powerful. However, simply and always present: through a touch or a word or a smile from a person, perhaps in church, who shares your faith and hope in a merciful God.

This morning a woman slipped into the pew beside us. She handed Fritz a teal green "healing shawl." She and a group of knitters pray for people in need while they work making shawls. They only know of Fritz's physical illness. We know, there is more to healing than getting well; some ills have no cure. All knowledge and willpower aside, we cannot get past this stumbling stone alone. So we wrap ourselves in the soft shawl, with a cross woven into its pattern—a visible reminder of God's eternal, warm and loving embrace.

1/9/12

Home in winter

Never Spar About the Small Stuff

We argued all the way home on our long drive from church. It began with me at the wheel and saying offhand, "I find it hard to concentrate on the sermon while sitting farther back in the church." After years of sitting within the first third of the sanctuary, Fritz decided we should sit toward the back. It began when he returned to church after his cheek operation. Perhaps it had something to do with getting out quicker at the end and avoiding socializing on the way. But, no, he still goes to the Fellowship Hall for coffee and conversation after the service.

Gauging his reaction to my statement, one would think a suggestion had been made to move to the very front pew.

He began to talk about the differences between us, but not my preference to be a little closer to the podium. "You are outgoing and I am not; you are comfortable talking in front of groups and I am not." Following that argument, he mentioned a familiar theme: "You know how hard it was for me to lecture when I was a professor, practicing the night before until knowing the lecture backward and forward. This hasn't changed, and now I hate to speak to groups." Still protesting I assured him my sitting a little closer to the front had nothing to do with speaking publicly.

He went on—telling his distain for people who "parade up to the front row." It never occurred to me that slipping into the eighth pew back was a parade. It was more like a tradition. Bringing the subject up was the basis for my preference with a clear sight of the pastor and a sense that what she says was directed my way.

Fritz ran out of ideas for rebuttal and repeated the old points again. Instead of answering any of my questions he went off on the same tangent, raising his voice and clearly getting upset. I said, "You have brought up some interesting subjects, but let's just drop it."

He would not and said if I wanted to "parade" up front then he would sit in the back, alone. It is difficult not to react to accusations like that. Turning quiet again, I finally said, "As long as you are going to church, we will sit together." Nothing resolved; dumb argument.

Arguing is an art. It takes two people with opinions who exchange ideas and points of view. On our best days we used to do that well. Both of us had read, observed or talked to someone about a topic so that we were prepared. On many things we agreed so that real arguments were few—more like discussions. I'll always be grateful that we are on the same side of the religious and political fences. For the other things, even stupid little points, we were good "sparring partners." It is a mystery to me how that phrase was coined, but certainly I am the only one who used it in reference to the two of us. We've done our share of petty nit-picking, and sometimes not so privately. When they were fair fights, I called it sparring.

You must be close to equal to be "spar-ers." Otherwise one person has an advantage going in that makes it unfair. We may have begun our private sparring over the issue that most stuck in my craw: the role of women in the church and society. Even though he was on my side and the side of all striving women, he would often bait me—pretending to agree with other guys, who held very traditional views. Maybe he was helping me get my talking points in order. He knew any failure on my part to articulate my stance or my cause, would be easily put down. During a certain era, women had to be ready when the opposition tried to discredit their womans' points of view.

Fritz could argue well back then; seeing all sides and fashioning his response to fit even a rapid exchange. That trait was often key to his selection as the leader in several committees. The skill of negotiation, after all sides were heard, belonged to him. Mild mannered but forceful was his way of dealing with stickier issues among very opinionated scientists.

We can no longer have a fair fight, so I must stop myself before a potential argument arises. A quick exchange of opposing opinions leaves him in the dust. His memory does not let him keep the train of an argument flowing; it gets stuck on the first thought. Repeating that one thought may sound irrelevant, however, it his only defense. I should be

Fritz and Carol on steps of Old Yellow House (Marble)

glad that he still wants to spar. It has been an important part of our life together. I have to learn how to fight fair with a wounded opponent.

1/23/12

You Have to Be There

We always watch the PBS News Hour. Fritz was very impressed by an interview with Karl Pillemer, about his book: *30 Lessons for Living.* The author proposed that instead of going to the so-called experts we should ask our questions about living well from the real experts: older people who have done just that. "Will you order that for me?" he asked, knowing about my rather direct line to Amazon.com. Eyeing his other "must have" books sitting untouched, my question was, "Are you sure you will read it?" He convinced me that this one sounded really good, so I followed his orders.

When the package came, including a second book to cancel the shipping costs, he watched me open the box. Fritz wanted to know who ordered the books. With a smile, my response was, "One is for you and one is for me." He did not remember anything about the book. By then my memory could not quickly bring to mind where the idea for the book originated. After reading a few lines, I remembered the context. It was written in a straightforward way and could be read in chunks, so I urged him to pick it up. Several more times, when he saw the book lying near his chair, he wondered aloud "WHO bought this book?"

I'm asked to remember the circumstances and the details about everything from books within reach, to whom he might have talked to, to what we ate for supper last night. In other words, I have to be there, beside him, seeing and hearing the same things, or they will be lost.

Phone calls get lost. If someone calls, he will forget to tell me. The kids know this now, and often preface the next call with "Did Dad tell you that I called?" "No, but what was on your mind?" Urging him to write down the caller's name or subject is not the answer. Often he wrote too much or too little—all of which is confusing. It took my careful deciphering of disjointed comments or words before returning calls.

Saturday night he wanted me to go to the book club meeting without him. He had not read the book and did not have the energy to enjoy standing around talking and eating and then concentrating on a complicated discussion. So I went, enjoyed myself and didn't feel rushed. On the way home, a call to Fritz let him know we would soon be together. "So late?" he asked the minute I walked in the door. Was he uneasy being alone or just at a loss about what to do next? Reading TV schedules and finding the right station was getting harder. Breaking tradition—harder. We usually sat together in the living room—he watching and I reading or playing Scrabble against the computer. Always just close enough to get him out of any quandary.

A better time for me to be away was when someone else was at the house with him. Son-in-law Dave offered now and then to come and help. They did well together and my time spent away was relaxing. Others can help in ways that I cannot. Besides—I smell freedom.

Helping our son Doug with meals and handling papers, often left me torn about just where to be. Timing my visits to Doug's between lunch and supper cut down on the angst at home. Not appearing when Fritz thinks it is time, made him mad or floundering for direction.

At another time of our lives, I might have just walked out of the house with a breezy, "Find something in the fridge for lunch." Now Fritz does not eat much, unless we are together. He never had very good search instincts, but now the fridge must look like a jumble. Long ago, before we retired, the kids latched onto their dad's most common phrase, "Where abouts, Carol?" When looking for an item, no amount of direction could lead him to it. He always wanted the TV guide where it could be easily found. Often, he wanted me to search it for him. To him the refrig and the viewing grid must look like just more puzzles.

Not much of Fritz's confusion was evident to people we met. His demeanor was always pleasant as when he joined the discussion, sometimes even asking a pertinent question. If there was an opening after a remark was made, he added to the topic. If not, his observation might come quite out of context. The more people talked the more confusing it became. If we were together, I kept him on track by slipping something in that connected the recent point to what he had said.

Back to that book he forgot he wanted. The first section dealt with long-term marriages. One point made was about giving each other the freedom to have independent interests and activities. Fritz and I have always prized independence, even as we enjoyed depending on each other for so much of our day-to-day lives. I think we have been a good team because we found "spaces" where each could thrive alone.

Another point made in *Thirty Lessons* was about the give and take in marriage. You can't, said the wise older folks, expect this to be a fifty-fifty deal. Each partner needs to give more than his or her fair share—one hundred percent available to give if needed!

Several times lately, Fritz has told me how much he appreciates all that I do for him. He knows I am picking up the slack, when he is tired or forgetful or needs help navigating his computer. He says wistfully that he really wants to do something for me—while he still can. I tell him that he has always been ready to give me and others, his time and talent.

I don't say the rest of what I am thinking: he still gives generously, but dementia has taken away much of what he has to give. His gifts to me may be fewer, but they are still one hundred percent, everything he has.

1/23/12

Don't you dare get sick...

Everywhere robotic clerks send me off with a variation of the cheery, "Have a good day." I think, *If you only knew what one day could bring.* This journey with my husband began with resolve to take "one day at a time." I have always lived that way—optimistic by nature. But things change; fear enters uninvited.

One fear is getting sick. Incapacitated even for a short-time I might be unable to cook or drive to his radiation appointments. However, fear has not stopped me from neglecting all the things that could keep me healthy: regular exercise, balanced diet, regular preventive visits to my doctor and dentist, outlets for my passions. The other day I finally got a flu shot, at the urging of my husband. His reasoning, he can't afford to catch anything from me. My reasoning, if I get sick, I can't take care of him. My sore arm and a lingering headache from the vaccine was a sign of just how tied together we are in health and in sickness.

Fritz shouldered most of the sickness except for my one long period of internal bleeding almost half a life ago. We were in our early forties—he was healthy and resourceful; our children, helpful teenagers. After several months of hospitalization, I slowly climbed back to health, with my body eventually recovering full strength. I had taken up running a few years before and was able to resume. Several years ago, pneumonia followed me home from Africa—nothing that rest and medications and the attention of a loving husband could not cure.

Fritz's medical chart is fat: prostrate cancer, an organ transplant, skin cancer, knee, shoulder and hand surgeries and now dementia. Through most of it we have been

In Kenya

partners dealing with the symptoms, seeking help, facing the inconveniences, side effects and eventually wellness. He has endured much pain and uncertainty. I was always his sounding board and go-fer, but never his nurse.

Unlike three of my "nurse-siblings," I would have made a terrible nurse. Although my bedside manner is poor, it has been called upon several times. Two years after my bleeding bout, my injured son required home care. When the two of us tried to accomplish a task we would get caught up in conversation and forget what had to be done. Efficient I am not.

Now deterrents include more satisfying things, which I would like to be doing. Writing time at my desk, an activity that could satisfy me into old age, is so chopped up it is hard to know where to begin. I wish for an automatic "resume" button like we have on the TV recordings. This would let me know immediately and precisely where my writing left off. No more wasted time getting back on task. During considerable re-entry time it is easier to check the email, Google News or Facebook—all of which further sidetracked me. Concentrating on anything large or scholarly is almost impossible.

Providing physical help is still easier to perform than emotional help. When it comes to the big issues, when Fritz is unable to look forward to hopeful days—that is daunting. My sister-in-law has suffered with depression most of her life. She warns me the worst thing is to tell a depressed person to think of all their blessings and start being happy. So my job is to dissuade him with distractions, diversions and humor. If I let his moods overtake my own, this would be a very gloomy place.

Staying well is more than physical, although that seems to be my present concern. Friends have said that I look stressed; when I honestly look in the mirror I know they are right. As I write this, my back and shoulders tighten. Several weeks ago, I vowed to call for appointments: dentist, yearly physical and the foot doctor. It is embarrassing to say the first was the hardest—not only because I hate the dentist, but because my last appointment was three years ago! Now a toothache has forced the issue. The dental x-rays may show what I feel.

An hour later I had clean teeth and a NO cavities sticker. I wanted to surprise my mom like a kid with good news. The foot doctor looked at an old problem and ordered me to wear sneakers with a lift around the house. Next was the internist. Theresa is a great doctor and I always look forward to my yearly well-elder exam. She declared that I was very healthy and would probably live to a ripe old age, so I'd "better take care of myself." On the take-home report, one item said it all, "caregiver stress."

Driving to his daily radiation treatments is not stressful; staying home would be. He suggested on Friday, after five of thirty treatments on his cheek and neck, that he could probably drive himself. That won't happen. So far he has not been able to navigate off the freeway at the right spot, to park in the lot, go up the elevator to the right floor, get into the treatment reception area where parking tickets are stamped and ID's needed—alone. Afterward, he would have to follow the same pattern in reverse. When your memory cannot be relied upon, each step could lead to misery.

I'll do my best to stay well so I can continue to remember for two. So buck up and practice what you preach: one day at a time, don't anticipate troubles, and think of distractions to trick both of us into the possibility of "having a good day." Maybe we'll stop at his favorite store, Lowe's on the way home.

2/6/12

Everyone loves the sound of a train in the distance...

The only thing we can be sure of is change. Just how that change comes about is as erratic as the change itself. When I think of adjusting to a major change, I imagine it to be gradual with one thing leading to another. Like one of those long escalators that carry you up from the airport baggage level to the loading area. Once on the moving stairway, you don't go back, you just rise. If you are going down, it is a one-way staircase. Occasionally we see kids trying to go up a

Grandparents with twin grand babies, Brian and Marielle—1997

down escalator, but it is a losing proposition. Looking back over life-changes from the perspective of years, they seem more gradual than what we are experiencing today.

I thought dementia would be like riding on a downward trajectory. Maybe it would not be one long escalator, but a series of them leading from one level to another like those in a large department store or mall. There would be a chance to stop at a level, look around and get the lay of the land before continuing down. If any one level was pleasing, stay there for as long as possible. This was the hope offered in the use of memory medications. Someone recently asked me what "level" my husband was at. Just like "stages of grief," levels seem handy for clinicians for charting but seldom work in real life.

Memory loss and all that comes with it seems more like a passenger train with many cars. Every car is like a box of change, which is attached by a coupling device to the one ahead and behind. Passengers can walk from one car to another and, if necessary, go back to the car from which they came. Occasionally a "car" is locked, like the food car after hours, preventing passage; but mostly there is wandering from one to the other.

Dementia's change is not gradual or orderly. It does not give you time to adjust to one set of circumstances before it moves to the next. If you think you are going to be there for a while, there may be a reversion to an earlier ability or the loss of routine skill. Just when you think you know what to expect, the unexpected happens.

Most days when I go to my husband's study, the untidy state of things represents the chaos in his mind. The unorganized papers and other items call to him from every angle. Little Post-it Notes hanging on the computer screen, three glasses of water, stacks of unrelated papers and upright files. He often calls me to get him out of an email mess. Each day, he laments that he is just not efficient any more. Then, without notice—his desk is straight and he looks like a calm and self-satisfied professor. What changed? Will it last?

There must be a looping going on, like two steps back and one forward. Or, four steps back for a while, and then all the way to the front of the train. Sometimes I'm tempted to think that the diagnosis is all wrong and we must have imagined the decline to be worse than it really is. That hopefulness just sits and waits for a good sign and then hangs on to it for dear life. We shuffle in and out of places of denial.

We have been to a lot of doctors lately. When discussing a problem, Fritz is attentive and asks good questions. The doctor and nurse have no idea that as soon as we leave, he will ask me what was said. And then a few minutes or an hour after that when I refer to something from the visit, he will say, sometimes accusingly, "You never told me that."

After getting a booklet about the possible side effects of the radiation he is presently getting, I condensed the symptoms and ways to address them on one sheet of paper. I gave him a copy. Not only did he not read it, he was also sure I never gave him a copy. Now he has his copy but continues to ask at each juncture, "What am I supposed to do now?" My hope for a little carryover from one situation to another has vanished. It is hard for me to remember that even repeat situations are new to him.

There are times when Fritz can rise to the occasion. If he remembers to have a nap and a cup of coffee before someone visits, he can carry on. When I do not expect it, he tells a long tale of some recent event with amazing clarity and detail. Could a pathway to memory be opening before our ears? But alas, about that time he tells a grandson of exploits with his aqua-lung when he was a boy of his age. I watch that knowing look on the child's face—*I could tell YOU this story, I have heard it so many times before.* Even if his grandson says, "Yea, you told me that," it does not stop grandpa from retelling the story just as it is imprinted on his mental tape recorder.

At the first sight of snow this year, Fritz was determined that he needed a new snowblower to replace the one that started hard. We have a plow service that leaves only a little snow on the last entry to the garage and the walkways. I protested the necessity, offering instead to promptly shovel where the plow failed to clear. Instead he followed his heart to a blowing machine at Lowe's. We stopped two days in a row,

Doug's kids with grandparents in Marble

on the way home from radiation to make sure he asked all the right questions and made a good choice. The salesperson said they would load it on his trailer. When the time came for purchase, I let him go alone. What could go wrong? I would soon find out.

First, the clerk asked him if he had a Lowe's credit card. Fritz was sure we had one, but could not locate it. When he called me about the card, I assured him that we DID NOT have a Lowe's card. He called again saying he could get five percent off if he had one, and decided he would apply. I know how detailed those credit card applications can be but he was determined. Two more calls for bits of information as I could hear his anxiety level rising. I should never have let him go alone.

When he got home, he described the trip as "hellish." The salesman, the clerk and perhaps even other customers became impatient with him. The service he expected evaporated—he had to search for someone to load the snowblower, after all. For the sake of twenty-nine dollars he went through agony. His trip to Lowe's nudged my thinking: Change comes when change is least expected, Fritz is suddenly wandering from train car to train car.

Near our first house, there were railroad tracks on the south and the Red Cedar River on the north. At first, the abrupt whistle of that train startled me, day and night; later I began to love the sounds of the tracks singing and the whistle in the distance. Some vague longing spoke through that sound.

Years after all of us had moved away from the sound of the train, my son gave me a Paul Simon CD, with these lyrics in one chorus:

Everybody loves the sound of a train in the distance
Everybody thinks it's true
What is the point of this story?
What information pertains?
The thought that life could be better/ is woven indelibly/
into our hearts and our brains.

That longing thought beats daily in the distance; that is the point of my story.

2/16/12

Keeping Secrets

One of my children shared with me something terrible that happened in his/her family but as the words gushed out, added, "Don't tell Dad." Here I sit with a secret. This makes me feel very alone with a situation for which I can get no support, no listening ear. Because the one who shared the secret has cut off all my avenues—perhaps not aware of how hard it is for me to feel comfortable in this place.

The secret would have been shared with both of us, if Fritz were able to handle it. His old instincts of "fixing it" would have come out, even though neither he nor any of us are capable of fixing anything. He would obsess over it; he would ask endless questions for which there are no answers. He might even do something inappropriate which would make the situation worse.

After the upsetting phone call, it was important to continue to interact with Fritz as though nothing happened. I'm upset but I cannot show it. Otherwise Fritz will think that he did something wrong or that I am hiding something. He already thinks that I am keeping information from him, that he has a "right" to know. Certain delicate situations in the family require that we control our feelings for the sake of the children. While most of us have moved on from our disappointment and hurt, my husband has not. Right now he knows enough not to express his feelings openly—but will he lose those inhibitions in time?

If he were well, there would be no question about sharing everything. We spent so many years depending on each other to deal with certain stresses and lend a shoulder to cry on. Secrets like these stayed in the family, but they were never mine alone. Though no one has told me not to, I choose to not share even more things with him. His judgment is impaired. It always astounds me that faulty cognition affects so many things.

Judgment: when and how to act in the case of an emergency have been tested lately. The first instance was when a slight blip in the electricity interrupted the cycle of the furnace. It was a cold day, and Fritz was sure that the furnace was not working. He repeatedly wanted me to feel the air coming from the duct—not even warm, he said. We checked the furnace, which sported one flashing green light. Having never involved myself with the heating/cooling I did not know what was normal. Fritz could not remember and insisted we call the repair person immediately. I said wait; he said no. The man came—there was no problem since the furnace just goes through a cycle once it is interrupted. By the time the repair person came, the heat was flowing as usual. All was not lost—I now know what is normal and more about furnace operations.

Then came the flood. Fritz decided the dog needed a bath but the shampoo bottle was too sticky. He came inside, threw the bottle in the laundry room tub and turned on the water. Then he went to watch his beloved Spartans play basketball. I don't know if he meant to plug the sink; I don't know how long the water overflowed before I heard the gurgling sound. But by that time warm water was gushing over the sides, onto the floor and also, I soon learned, dripping from the ceiling below, covering the basement floor and the workbench. You get the picture—a soggy, sloshy mess.

It takes judgment to decide what to do about such a mess. His old instincts to solve the problem rushed in, even though he was mentally and physically compromised. He would not reason with me about a solution—just went headlong into crisis mode. He could not find the water vac and was sure "someone" had taken it. His anger at "someone" clouded his reasoning further. I worked with towels and mops but he had a better, quicker way. Meanwhile, the Big Ten championship rolled on without us.

When you spend your adult life being the leader of household repairs, you never expect to have to follow the guidance of another. And that other—me—really never thought about having to work through these things herself. All things mechanical were relegated long ago. I don't know if it will be easier as time goes on when he no longer knows a problem exists but can't imagine a time he will not offer advice. I look at emergencies in new ways—learning as much as possible along the way. And—keeping mental notes of where records are stored and making a list of all those repair persons that will soon be hearing from me, not the man of the house.

And back to those secrets I've been entrusted with—I don't like keeping them. Writing this makes me feel like I have somehow betrayed my faithful confidant. It must be like lying during the war to save an innocent person. There is no peace in doing what you must do—no satisfaction in taking over jobs for which you are ill equipped. For a while you must do what is necessary and pretend that you did nothing and know nothing. I pray for no more secrets and no more heat or water surprises. Life is messy; is more of the same waiting?

3/14/12

The farmer

CHAPTER SIX

CHANGEABLE WEATHER: CLOUDS AND SUNSHINE

Sunday Pain

The radiation treatments were finished, and on a Saturday night Fritz decided it was time for him to go back to church. He was rather firm about it, except for a few caveats about the possibility of canceling at the last minute. I didn't urge him to go but let it be based on how he felt.

Sunday morning his hands were shaking when getting his things together. In the car he snapped about a few small things; then we went on in silence. Doug called a few minutes into the drive about some details concerning the house he was buying. My cell phone goes through the car speaker so Fritz was listening and also responding. Doug raised a matter and I tried to address it. But Fritz wanted to talk about something different: offer to buy furniture the departing owners do not want. He did not remember that the furniture purchase was a done deal.

After the call, he took exception to what transpired. He expressed the belief that he was being left out of many things. In a kind of paranoia, he said, "I am not as smart as I used to be, but I still want to be involved." He felt slighted and no amount of reassurance from me changed his mind. My thick skin thinned in a hurry and prompted me to rise to my own defense. I should have known better. Suddenly he stopped talking, maybe thinking ahead to the next hurdle. He seemed to calm the closer we got to our destination.

Soon we were sitting in the pew he chose close to the exit. All seemed fine. A friend came over to greet him and another stopped when he'd finished ushering just to welcome him back. They were just quick—"good to see you" kinds of messages. The service, like so many before, varied with music and The Word, and a wonderful sermon about Sabbath rhythm. Our return resumed a rhythm that had sustained both of us for so long. We held hands for part of the service as we often did. Then, toward the end, I could feel his slight inner shaking. That should have been my clue. Maybe his "blood was boiling" as it sometimes does for all of us when experiencing anger or stress or uncertainty.

As we left the pew he said he wanted to go. No argument from me as we steered toward the nearby door. Several people acknowledged his welcomed presence, and a close friend rushed over with a gentle greeting. There was stress all over Fritz's face. In the car, he expressed his regrets for coming. I assured him that this was an important first step even though it must have been very hard.

On the way home his feelings spilled out: discouragement most of all at the slow pace of his recovery. Then, he said, "It must be hard on you too, not being able to socialize after the service." I brushed that off, saying there would be plenty of time for that later. But as the trip wore on his remarks became hurtful, not thoughtful—just a jumble of emotions misdirected toward me. He brought up the house/

furniture again as a clear violation of his place in decision-making. He declined my offers to stop for a soft drink; his mouth was dry causing more stress. Then he fussed about the little compartment between the front seats being a mess and needing to be cleaned—as if by a miracle, in the clutter, was a can of Sprite. It was quickly consumed. The sugar and the moisture restored one kind of balance in his body and mind. No such elixir for me. Still under the cloud of misunderstanding, blame and dread, once at home and changing clothes in the walk-in closet, I began to cry. He was right behind me.

Tears always stop the action. In response to his questioning eyes came my feeble cry for understanding, "I'm not always strong." I can't blame him for things beyond his control. In his present state he rarely saw the plight of the other and thought it was always about him. Once again he took me on with arguments about the same subjects that had occupied us to and from worship, although the cause of his stress was altogether different. I wished he hadn't seen my tears.

He was suddenly tired of everything—the house, his desk, the NCAA tournament, life—and wanted to get away. My suggestion was our usual Sunday afternoon walk in the woods, but he said he was "not too bubbly." The day before he said something similar about his mental powers, "I'm not too spicy." His answer to unrest today was to drive miles through the country to see the Croton and Hardy Dams—a memory from his childhood. I didn't put up a fuss, even though the last thing I wanted to do was more driving. I wanted to make him happy. No, I wanted him to be happy. Jumbled thoughts ramble through my brain. I long for some Sabbath rhythm as we rode in silence for hours.

There is private pain in all of this. My physical sign of overload is suddenly going cold, shivering inside and looking for a sweater. It may be a sign of despair, much different than the boiling of anger. I want someone to wrap his arms around me and tell me it is going to be all right.

My evening calls to the kids do not include spilling today's sadness into their lives. What can they possibly do with my pain? It should be enough for me to know they are there. I have always tried to be strong for them. One day I will admit what they already know, "I am not always strong…"

3/26/12

Just a Little Spark

Our moods rise and fall many times during a day. His are never very high; I guess mine are morphing downward behind his. Tonight after supper he said dutifully, "I guess I'll go down to the work room again." From across the room my fist bump is telegraphed with his bump back to me. He smiles for the first time today.

His mornings generally start out lousy. He sleeps for eight hours or more. His first exertion, either breakfast or a shower, has him dragging his tail—so tired of being tired. Coffee and a muffin will revive him a little, so I bring both down to his desk. Sometimes he is praying; sometimes staring into space. He is always discouraged.

He doesn't really want me to leave. I finally break away, walk the two flights to my desk and my work. Everyday something new, or something old with a new twist. Part of his tiredness right now is due to overwork the day before. He has garden/yard help but wants to work alongside the helper. It is a noble desire but pays for it in extra fatigue the next day.

I worry about his negative self-talk. Being teased about my "silver-lining" attitude and a broad-based optimism is a thing of the past. I still look for the bright side, just to keep myself going. He dwells in the negative—"I am not efficient," "I should be able to ____," and the saddest of all, "I think I am going downhill."

The radiation treatments following tumor removal set us back. We dutifully trudged downtown daily for six weeks. Fritz mustered just enough energy to ride there, put on a happy face while being treated for fifteen minutes and then ride home. He lost his taste and appetite, his sense of humor—any sense of well-being he'd gained since the surgery.

Now at seven weeks post radiation, not much has changed. He is by times very tired and by times depressed. Generally as the day progresses he gains more strength. So the little spark this evening is a good sign. And for that reason alone, his little smile sent me soaring. He just sits on his stool by the workbench, puttering with his tools—organizing, as is his style, very slowly. He is getting something done—always the joy of his life.

4/26/11

I Am Happy

At church today, I told a friend that I was happy—happier than I have been in a long time. He smiled, perhaps remembering my downcast expressions for the last several months. What changed? I could not put my finger on it. Fritz drove us home, the first time in ages he has wanted to be the driver. But after walking in the door, he plopped down in his easy chair. He handed me the Sunday paper and asked me to find "something good on TV," his old default when not knowing what to do. His difficulty reading the TV Guide means I must wade through the listing using his sensibilities as my guide. If I just name some, he rejects them out of hand. Unfortunately, the guide only gives show titles; it doesn't explain their content. "You'll just have to find something," I said, handing back the controller.

While eating our sandwiches, I fussed when he was stuck on one of those awful infomercials, so he switched to another default, CNN. To our surprise, Dr. Sonjay Gupta was the host, leading three interviews, the clarity and interest of which were remarkable in the world of 24/7 Breaking News. At one point during the talk, Fritz mentioned a good article he'd read in the latest *Time* magazine about the background of finding Osama Bin-laden a year ago. I picked up the magazine to find the three-page spread, which contained very few pictures. "You read all of this?" I asked. "Yep, it was very interesting—you should read it too!"

Sandwiches gone, we turned off the tube when I announced it was time to go upstairs to finish the last few pages of my book, *Letters from the Land of Cancer*, by Walter Wangerin. In minutes Fritz called up to me asking where to find our next book club selection, *Social Animal*, by David Brooks. That was to be my next read, but I trundled it down to him. We had both looked at the red book jacket as it sat under our glass-topped coffee table for the last six months. Taking it he remarked about how big and heavy it was and how he'd never be able to finish it. "Just give it a try," I urged, "At least read the intro and you'll see the author's premise and where he wants to take you."

My skepticism kicked in. He has opted out of the last two club meetings—not even willing to go to listen to the discussion. He hasn't completed a book for over a year. This is a man who read scientific articles for a career in research, unable to let any new trend in his field go unnoticed. The complex data became part of his psyche without notes. He used the information to formulate experiments to search for the next "unknown." Dementia has changed all of that. His interest in science has become that of a layperson, and one that cannot remember the facts, or be able to bring up the vocabulary to share in casual conversation.

As I closed the cover of the *Land of Cancer*, with tears in my eyes, I heard some laughter from the dining room below. There was Fritz at the table reading the tome by columnist David Brooks, probably the only conservative he can tolerate, and being genuinely amused by his writing. I sat across the table and enjoyed his delight. He read me parts and laughed again.

My next book was, *When I Was Young I Read Books,* by Marilyn Robinson—a serious read, that demanded my full attention. I could hardly keep my place, as Fritz wanted to share passage after passage. Now and then, he would consider the size of the book and repeat that he'd never be able to read it all. He opened the book at random and began to laugh again at some disconnected passage. Back to his real place, he used a pencil to underline and a pad next to him on which to keep notes about what he read. "I'll stick with this for another half-hour and then let's go for a walk." Fair enough—if he can last that long, I thought. He went longer. When he finally got up, I wondered if a nap was more appropriate than a walk. He had clearly taxed his brain and was probably as tired as if he had run five miles. But he brushed aside my concerns and opted for a walk. I imagined his brain dancing happily inside his head. We talked of many things.

Suddenly I realized my husband had come back to life. To the life we knew in the past—sharing ideas, considering provocative writing, teasing out plots. And then: more sharing while walking about in the fields and woods considering the new spring blooms, the location of the swan's nest, the size of the skunk cabbage and all things native.

He never took that nap. After a light supper while watching "60 Minutes," he decided to read a little more in *Social Animal*. An hour later, he is still there reading away. My hope is that this will last. I have missed his sharp mind even more than his strong arms.

Why was I overcome with happiness today, even before this happened? Where in the music or sermon or scripture did I catch the hope that things could be different? Like foreshadowing in fiction, I got a hint from somewhere. My realistic heart fears that this is nothing more than fantasy. But I can't help but hear the sound of that train in the distance.

I will follow every nuance of our story line in hopes it will be a very long book. Or stop short of reading the last chapter, as I once did with good novels. Maybe then, it will never end.

Happy Birthday, Fritz
White Tulip

His only gift a wilting tulip
Plucked hastily
Lay beside his place
on the Birthday table.

An impromptu party
marking seventy-five years

Of living well
On this good earth.

Two children, three grandchildren
And me
Honoring our elder
Cheering his renewed health.

The youngest begged for old stories
Of peddling papers
Of never taking school books home
Of pranks played on blind Albert Bush.

Amid hugs and happy good-byes,
Well-wishes for their spring break,
The flower child reminded him
"Don't forget the white tulip!"

The bedraggled bloom
Looked beyond revival
Wrinkled and curling
on our kitchen counter.

Maybe, said I,
With a little water
And loving wishes
It will straighten again.

We cheered its gradual resurrection
Like an old white-haired man
Standing tall again
Perfectly whole.

3/30/12

With President Carter at the Carter Center, Atlanta

I Want to Talk About the Hard Stuff

A friend from Wyoming called and left a message: "Barb and I would like to come out to see you and Fritz." Larry is a family friend, who went to school and church with me back home in the 50s. I'd seen him from time to time; we greet as old friends with warm hugs. I don't know Barbara well, but she is the pretty woman by his side, greeting us with a ready smile and soft blue eyes.

Larry had a special purpose for the visit: he recently heard from a mutual friend about Fritz's dementia. Barb has dementia too. Hers is of a familial type; her two older sisters are at various stages in the disease progression. In his usual way Larry is taking the initiative in searching out people like us who are facing the same challenges.

Fritz was eager for the visit. I was worried. After all my thinking about navigating social situations with my husband, I was suddenly on the other side of the fence and wondering how to handle interactions with Barb. How do two couples talk about the disease that is eating away at the very relationship between husband and wife?

Larry has always been resourceful. He takes the lead—as I would soon learn during our casual conversation. We did not talk about Alzheimer's. He traced our places of residence and mentioned mutual acquaintances from parts of the country where we had resided. Barb sat demurely on the sofa, flashing her sweet smile now and then. Even if she could, there was no opening for her to add conversation. Fritz slipped in a few old stories; I added some bits from my old Denver perspective.

I offered a piece of pie just made from our garden rhubarb. They accepted and we moved to the kitchen table. Fritz warned that the pie might be too tart and they should not feel compelled to finish it. We laughed a bit and the atmosphere warmed. Larry asked if we had found good Alzheimer's resources in the area. Later, I thought about how odd that was. Up to that time no one had talked about the disease plaguing us. The "A" word had not been spoken. All the while, Larry and I were sizing each other up based on that knowledge. He brought a normalcy to the situation by making it a discussion point at just the right time, as we all finished every crumb of the pie.

They talked about their support group in Jackson Hole, and what it meant to them. I traced our efforts to find support and information. "Did the early dementia group feel good to you, Fritz?" Larry asked, giving Fritz an opening. Fritz was so positive; I wished we were still in that supportive group, so I could see that side of him again.

Once we were comfortable together, Larry became my sounding board. My question, "Have you made advanced directives based on what you know about the disease?" He is a retired doctor who must have thought about the eventualities of treatment for physical ills when Barb's mind barred the recognition of people she loved. But no—he spoke of plans for cremation and having their ashes commingled in an urn.

The time was not right for me to ask my most urgent questions: "Hasn't Barb mentioned often that if she got 'that bad' she didn't want to live? On days when nothing was going right, did she wish for the end? Did she, like Fritz, think of impossible plans to drive or bike or wander off into the sunset and never be heard from again? Had Larry considered the possible dilemma that he or his children would face when asked if she should be resuscitated or tube fed or intubated to prolong her life?"

Fritz and I have had those talks. He wants nothing to prolong his life. Even with that firm choice, the future is not ours to know. The possibility that one day I will have to make those decisions—haunts me. Fritz does not want to be a burden to himself or our family. If he is diagnosed with a serious illness, at what point do I make a conscious decision not to intervene because his life is no longer meaningful to him? To treat is so much easier than not to treat even though it means deferring a decision. If his heart or borrowed kidney fails, what will I do?

Grandson's Chris and Matt Lead King Basin

What I wanted from Larry were hints on how to navigate the health care system when the time comes. It seems that a living will, never completely covers such eventualities. There are always human decisions—ours, and the doctors. I'm reading a book called, *Decide While You Can*, by Dr. Colleen Tallen. I'm certainly not the first one to think ahead about these things.

Several hours pass quickly and they take their leave. We never talk about the hard stuff.

5/12/12

Time Between Times

"Maybe the time between times is the most difficult," our nephew mused in a private moment. We were spectators at his daughter's college graduation during our little conversation. We had just left the brothers, his father and my husband, at their house to keep each other company while we attended the long graduation ceremony. Fritz is younger by seven years, but diagnosed with dementia before his brother, Jack. Fritz is more physically able but both have growing limitations of thought. I can't help wondering what they are talking about. Fritz would only say afterward, "Jack doesn't talk very much." Their one remaining sibling, the oldest brother, lives in a nursing home and has similar limitations.

This week one thing struck me: we are entering into a new season of this illness. This is the time between forgetfulness and mental fatigue leading to a time of inability to plan ahead, remembering coming events and anger at people and things that do not work. Last week it was the sprinkler heads in the garden. After three trips to the distributor, he was still frustrated. Anger at the complicated water system, anger at the gas pump that he couldn't get to work, anger at me for suggesting that there might be a different way of looking at the problem. He criticized me for being on the phone or gone longer that he would like and the haircut I gave him and now being unable to comb his hair the way he always has. Each of these might seem just a little quirky but when piled up in a day, they are hard. He feels the pain of being left out of decision making but too limited in his ability to weigh possibilities.

Also this week was his six-month checkup with the neurologist. When asked how he thought he was doing, he said, "Today is a good day." He said nothing of all the complaints he had prior to the appointment and how many times he asked about the time. The doctor could read through the rosy words and see how he was functioning. I didn't have to say too much—several times I let Fritz go on and on without supplying the word that would make his comments understandable. He talked of physical ills—not discerning that this doctor was interested in his brain not his bladder. Also about fatigue—both the doctor and I knew that mental fatigue can be as tiring as physical tiredness and that they sometimes go together. In the end he recommended a higher dose of one medicine if his system could tolerate it. Ironically, one side effect has to do with the bladder!

Making plans is the stuff of calendars and arranging ones life so as to fit in the things that matter. Recently we were walking down the driveway discussing a conflict in plans for today— the afternoon graduation ceremony with dinner celebration following or an evening book club. He made the suggestion that we skip the dinner with relatives so that we could go to the book club meeting. He had read some of the book and seemed eager to go prepared, for a change. So I made the plans.

In the morning he fussed over the sprinkler again. I warned if he put in so much energy trying to fix the hose he would be worn out for the rest of the day. "It will only take a few minutes," he said. Hours later, as his frustration rose, my directive to "stop" was too late. He needed a nap, lunch and time to dress. The hour remaining was not enough. We had to be at the graduation when it began and left the house in a dither. I endured the sparks—not necessarily directed at me but filling the little car during the long ride. He questioned having to go and for having made what he now considered complicated plans.

Riding the Hobie-Cat at Glen Arbor

Perhaps that is the reason I had to write today. His moods are like a nuclear leak. You can't see it in the air, even while it is infiltrating your system. It is a poison that works its way in before you can calculate the damage that it is doing. As one incident resolves, sometimes with an apology, it leaves an invisible scar. It takes so much effort to move on when there is this residue of sludge and dread.

Will his personality change as his powers decline? Will he act on his anger about things that do not work or people who do not understand him? Will he lose his way because he is upset that a transaction went wrong? Does this mean I should go with him wherever he goes? I am not sure but I am afraid.

This may be the most difficult time—the time between being marginally well and too overwhelmed by the disease to care what is happening around him. For me, a time of not knowing what is coming around the bend. The present is hard enough.

Our nephew and his mother are walking on my same path but with different twists and turns. We share our pain as we feel the change. We know that the newness we observe from the outside is nothing like the mental chaos the brothers' feel from the inside. There is no way to glimpse inside Fritz's mind. He cannot express it. That old nuclear fallout just seeps in and robs. I can't let this time between times make me dull

Naum girls at Glen Arbor with Grandpa and Grandma

Tori and Grandpa in garden

to the significance of any of his revealing words and gestures. They may be the last windows into his soul.

5/21/12

Because you like to!

There was a time when I playfully described our family gardening efforts: he plans and plants; I pick and cook. The arrangement worked well for many years partly because I know very little about gardening while Fritz seems to have a built-in farmer's psyche. He's "in-tune" like a musician who knows when the pitch is perfect. He feels the rightness or wrongness of certain agrarian actions in his whole being.

My early gardening experience was my father planting wildly and then leaving the work to us kids. The garden always looked like a mess and hours of hard work in the Colorado sun never made a dent. I vacillated between guilt at not keeping it up and anger that he had planted it in the first place. The strawberries were good if you could find them in the overgrown patches.

I love the beauty of Fritz's garden—especially in the early summer. To see his garden is a feast to my eyes. Just what it takes to keep it looking that way is a real eye-opener for me. If you weed continually it is not so bad. Go away for a few days or a week, and the weeds want to take over. Even without enough water, they inch their way into the rich soil and spread their tentacles widely.

The weather always takes on prime importance during the growing season. He regularly predicts doom for all living things if we don't do one thing or another at just the right moment, like before the rain. Frost, early or late, is our nemesis. We have covered plants so often we have a permanent stack of sheets and tarps on the ready. One can rarely cover plants in pleasant weather—rain, wind and cold, are a part of the dreaded picture. Many a time I would have let a certain plant freeze to death, but he forced us to the rescue. Saving just added to our abundance.

Pick and cook has always been good for me. Cooking with fresh produce is such fun. The garden in summer is like having a green grocer in my backyard. As Fritz got more efficient and his gardens more productive, picking his abundance meant looking for people to give it to. Raspberries and beans are the most labor intensive. They need to be picked on time or will go to waste. Friends like to pick, but have hesitated when we tell them you *must* come at a time prearranged. Too much produce has its consequences. It's been said world hunger could be eliminated if only we could figure out the distribution chain. I deal with that on a small scale.

Garden challenges come long before the first seeds are planted. Right after Christmas the seed catalogs begin coming. If we wait until February, Fritz predicts that all the good stuff will be gone because we are *so late*. But one of his favorite stories is about getting asparagus roots from Johnny's Seeds when a foot of snow still covered the garden. He wrote to complain, and they said, "Just keep the roots—we'll send you some more in a few months. When the time came to plant he put them all in—unsure of getting anything. He had tried and failed so often before and this timing glitch might be just one more failure. Lo and behold—all of the plants came up and we have had the most hearty patch of asparagus ever since!

Last year I noticed ordering seeds was becoming weighty for Fritz. It took him three days of thumbing the catalog, circling items, writing them on an order form and calculating the total. When his overwhelming confusion became more apparent, I finally rewrote the order form and tallied the amount due before mailing it in.

This year I have seen a dramatic turn with Fritz's garden. In spring he ordered his usual abundance of seeds from Johnny's—the same company that inquired if we were commercial farmers, because of the unusually large order we placed. So what, I thought, if we get many more seeds than we actually need—it seemed harmless enough. But now as I look at the box of seed packets, I find it a burden. Five varieties of carrots, two kohlrabies, pounds of bean and snow pea seeds, even peppers, which we buy as nursery plants.

The scientist in Fritz says that he likes to compare varieties so we know which one we like best. However, by the time we have that figured out the markers are lost or similar seeds have been planted right next to each other. The picker throws them into one basket without knowledge of the actual variety. There are no notes from last year saying, we liked this type most; order this. There are just many years of buying the same types. Every year is a repeat experiment.

When the order came, I sorted the seeds and attached a picture from the catalog to the packet so I could have a visual. I tried to arrange them by planting date based on experience with other years, but again without real knowledge. Fritz made his annual trip to Motman's in nearby Allendale for plants but kept them in the garage waiting for the right time to plant. There is a rule of thumb that Michigan's last chance of frost is before Memorial Day, but after an eight-day forecast of warmer than average temps, I pushed for planting. No! We had to wait. Then we got a late start because of other schedules.

The next hard part was deciding where in the ten-row-garden each type of veggie would be placed. Fritz made a diagram long ago that could be filled in as planting decisions materialized. Not being able to make head or tail of last year's entries, I started my own chart, suddenly realizing I would be planting the seeds with no more instruction than what could be read in small print on the packet. Meanwhile he was puttering with fences and nets, etc., seemingly unaware of my planting load. His two main functions as gardener-in-chief, planning and planting, had become mine. It didn't seem so bad until the second-guessing began. Why here, why so deep, why so thick, why, why, why?

My sense of ownership in "Fritz's garden," must remain a private joy, not a public one. When I gave some early produce to my daughter, she said "Tell Dad 'thank you'!" We have a helper one day a week, who works tirelessly to conform to Fritz's idea of perfection. Together we try to preserve his sense of accomplishment in the garden that has always meant so much to him. Fritz is quick to credit his paid helper, but not me, which must feel like an extension of his own labor. I bristle sometimes, but realize that shared accomplishment has been a mark of our marriage and we have never calculated who did more or less.

His chief preoccupation is getting rid of the varmints these days. When on the prowl for rabbits, moles, chipmunks, or bugs he seems oblivious of the other hard work of the garden. While I was on my knees one day, I challenged him, "Why do you think I am doing all this?" His response was swift, "Because you like to!" There was no hint that he saw me as anything but willing.

Long ago whenever he pressed me to "weed right now" as he anticipated some calamity, I would give him an hour before going back to *my work*. "Gardening is your hobby, not mine!" The time for that kind of boldness has passed.

I must say that my farmer's heart is growing stronger. Every morning checking the tender plants and deciding on what needs to be done—weeding, thinning, watering, picking. I am proud of what it has become. Cooking the produce has taken on added value. When visitors rave over the produce we share or how beautiful the growing vegetables look, I just say, "Fritz is a master gardener!"

5/30/12

Dying Slowly

My friend, Shirley, is dying. She is dying quickly. Several bodily systems are shutting down, limiting her movements and causing unpleasant consequences. Her living room has become an equipment jungle, with a hospital bed she can no longer use and a reclining chair that is better for sleeping. Wheelchair and walker clog the space once easily maneuvered, through great room to sunroom to deck. She and her husband Ken live on an inland lake in a house they had built three years ago on a steep incline of a hill. This is their retirement home. There are sixty steps down to the lowest of three levels before meeting the trail down to the water. There is only one thing wrong with the beautiful home—it demands mobility.

A month ago, Shirley and Ken decided to end treatment for her cancer. She was in the hospital after her kidneys shut down. Her rare cancer had metastasized to her liver about a year before. They tried every mainstream and experimental trial that she qualified for. They traveled to Pennsylvania repeatedly for treatments, until the last chance experiment did nothing to reverse the course of her disease. In the hospital for the last time, after two rounds of dialysis, the doctor told Shirley that they could keep her alive for a while on dialysis but only in the hospital. They knew they were close to the end of the road. They chose to spend their last days together in their hillside home.

With hospice care, Shirley has remained comfortable for a little over a month. Neither Ken nor Shirley thought it would be that long, but they are thankful for the time they have. One daughter and their youngest grandchild have moved in, partly to create some normalcy. Friends like me bring a meal from time to time. We sit and chat, trying not to let our incredible sadness over her impending death spill over everything.

After talking to Shirley and Ken for a while, I took my leave when she showed signs of fatigue. Ken walked me up the steps toward my car. He is a man with a ready smile; he always looks happy on the outside. He is as frightened as Shirley, as death approaches. He admitted that his anger at God has surfaced at times. Why would God take someone so precious? He is unsure about his ability to survive without Shirley.

He knows about what is happening to Fritz. Ours is a different sort of fear: what does it take to die slowly? Neither Ken nor I can imagine the dilemma of the other. I remember my mother's expressed wish that her life would end the same way my father's had: heart attack while he slept. Contemplating death as a healthy woman approaching ninety, hers was a fear of the unknown—how, when and will it hurt. Thinking, as Ken and Shirley are doing right now, about death's relentless approach is difficult. They concentrate on taking joy in each day.

I find that thinking about death's slow, relentless movement, as in Fritz's dementia, is impossible. The days that one is supposed to take one at a time are too many. There are days of near normalcy when my mind quickly moves into the mode in which the future looks possible, even bright. Plans, decisions, hopeful thoughts creep back in. Until there is a "bad day" of confusion, anger at a machine that no longer works or my ignorance of the way he likes things to be done. I am constantly off-balance.

If I could watch, like Ken does Shirley, and see signs of physical decline, it might be easier. If Fritz's brain became transparent displaying clues about what the day would bring, that would help. To all observers, he is not dying any more than the rest of us on life's journey. People at church think he is doing fine. Our children get a longer view. However, they are often shocked at changes in just a few months. My view is the sporadic rise and fall—uneven yet decidedly earthward.

Shirley's approaching death is painful. Her body cannot withstand the cancer's destruction. She is clear of mind and bravely sits erect, making no apologies for her bald scalp or the disarray of the household. Once a week a social worker comes to record her life story. Shirley tells me she is only through her high school years and doesn't know how far she will get.

Ken would not wish to confront my future—the long road of demise. All the stories of Alzheimer's end with sadness. There may be difficult public embarrassment or trauma over wandering or loss of inhibitions. There may be years of caregiving. A man whose wife died recently of Alzheimer's told me cheerfully that he had "just lost his job." Caretaking had become a way of life for him. It had become his reason for existence even though his wife had not spoken for years.

One morning the call came from Ken. Shirley had died early that morning. All the kids got there, including their son from Pennsylvania. Shirley had time to tell him she loved him. It meant so much.

Our children may never know those kinds of last words. I never did because my father died in his sleep. Fritz is dying slowly and none of us are comfortable saying our good-byes now. Those of us who walk beside the slow death of a loved one with dementia never know when words uttered may be the last. When death approaches, those last words may have already flown away.

Fritz, Larry and Roland — at Snowmass Summit

Love expressed is never a loss. Now is the time to talk of love. When words are gone—we will still know that we have loved—and been loved—unuttered or expressed.

Early fall snow in Marble, Colorado

CHAPTER SEVEN

TWILIGHT

Vacation Time

Often when we are relaxing in front of the television, Fritz will remark that we should travel while we both feel well. Late afternoon and evening are his best times, when he can rise from his perpetual tiredness to some hopeful place. I love that place, especially after a morning of listening to complaints about aches and inefficiency, the kind of talk that gets me down. When he mentions wanting to travel somewhere beautiful, my heart leaps. I begin to dream again.

We start planning our annual trip to the Colorado Mountains, to Marble. What better place to enjoy the company of family? This year the two of us would fly out with our fourteen-year-old granddaughter, Tori, while the rest of the family drove. I decided we should fly into Aspen instead of Denver, which shortens the driving time from airport to cabin from four plus hours to a little over an hour.

During the week before departure, there was a lot of second-guessing. Throughout each incident of tiredness, Fritz said he couldn't possibly go to Colorado. If he could not walk at home, how would he fare at the higher altitude? "I'll be a drag to the whole family," he says. "What can I do while everyone else is active?" And thinking of last year, "What if I get sick again?"

Behind the scenes my daughter helped me plan for times when he could think of nothing to do. There is no television, no Internet or radio reception and he seems baffled by iPods. We got a new easier puzzle and made plans to listen to and write his stories using various recording scribes. Though we encouraged him at every turn, his doubt remained.

About three days before leaving when he talked again of bailing, I said, "You are going because if you don't I can't go either!" I put my foot down, just as with a child, trying not to wield authority but resolve. "We will deal with whatever comes."

On the morning of departure, the three of us left the house about six. After the flurry of packing, Fritz probably did not get much sleep. And for one who usually sleeps late, this was a huge stretch. I organized, drove, parked and got us into the waiting area for the plane on time. He worried.

The long flight to Denver from Grand Rapids was calm. One of my concerns was trying to get Fritz to eat periodically to keep his strength up. When I tried pushing a granola bar or fruit he insisted on waiting for "real food." Well, if you have ever tried to get fast food on a short layover in a busy airport you can guess what is coming.

We left him sitting in the waiting area and went to get him something to eat. Time was short so Tori went to one line and I chose another. We could see Fritz, but it was still a long and anxious wait for service I finally got him a hot dog and a banana because they were fast—nothing for myself. Before getting back to Fritz, our connecting flight to Aspen was called. Fritz's nervousness accelerated as the majority of the travelers checked in and Tori was still not back. It was a relief when she finally appeared and we could board the plane.

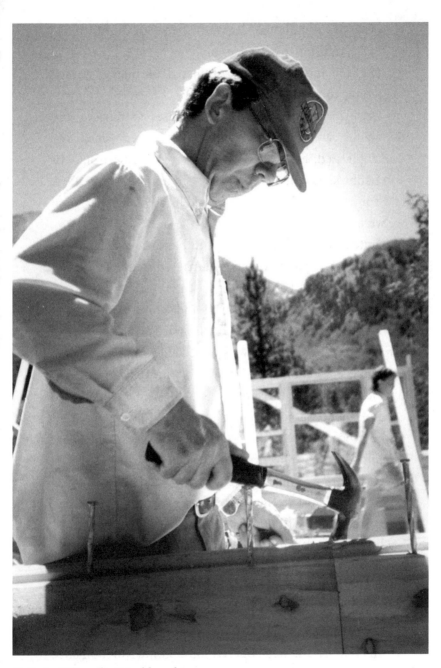

Fritz building the Marble cabin

Fritz sat the entire last leg of the trip with the lunch bag on his lap, refusing to eat it. He could not get over how foolish we had been and how we almost missed our flight. I wanted to grab the food and eat it myself.

Once in Aspen, there were suitcases to retrieve and the rental car to pick up. The airport is very small and uncomplicated. Fritz acted like we were in LaGuardia. His adrenaline kicked in but his energy had not been replaced. A bad combination. Finally we insisted he sit on a bench until we were ready to go.

Suitcases assembled and keys in hand we walked to the parking lot to find the car in a numbered stall. In this high altitude, he could hardly make it. The rental was a Toyota like ours so I had fewer unknowns and soon we were on our way out of the Aspen valley and on toward Marble. Fritz still refused to eat his lunch so we stopped at the first Wendy's to get him a shake and lunch for Tori and me. Finally he eased up and took some nourishment.

But there was one more hurdle. We needed to stop at the grocery store and stock up for the week. Any other year it would have been easy. After all, we had not driven cross-country overnight like the others and had not arrived physically exhausted. But we had the x-factor. Fritz insisted that he come in with us. He pushed a cart for support. But his hot dog nourishment gave out before the shopping trip. He asked if we had this or that item. Two minutes later the same questions, again. Our granddaughter had trouble understanding why her Grandpa could not remember more than two minutes.

In contrast, the week offered some wonderful moments: Grandpa interacting with his two nineteen-year-old grandsons about photography; looking at old pictures on the laptop; riding by jeep to one of his favorite spots, Lead King Basin, to see the wildflowers; attending the familiar Marble Community Church. Fritz surprised us all by his dogged determination to walk a loop from the cabin, up hill and then down, each day.

The rental car had to go back earlier than the flight so I promised Tori we would go by bus to Aspen to shop for a few hours. Fritz really didn't want to go but I could not leave him that long in the airport. When we got off the bus in Aspen he was already tired. After a McDonald's breakfast he wanted to stay sitting on a bench while we did our thing. We agreed to be in touch by cell phone.

When I called he did not answer; I hurried back to find him, but he was not there. I madly raced around the shopping area asking a few people if they had seen someone of his description. Tori waited at a shop several blocks away. A clerk said a man had asked her if there was a movie theater nearby. Could he be sitting in a movie? The tiny theater down the block was our best guess so we looked at times, movies and asked at the desk and the concession. Oh yes, a gray haired guy bought some popcorn. We waited at either exit. By some miracle, he appeared, carrying his uneaten popcorn. He wondered what all the fuss was about. Why would he sit on a hard bench when he could be sitting in a movie? Oh, Schipol, just like the first time I lost him. We headed back to the city bus, the day in ruins.

The flight back to Denver was short, enough time for food on the layover and then a blessed rest during the two plus hour flight home. We all had an unpleasant aftertaste about the trip. I made some costly mistakes in judgment. It is hard to anticipate how physical tiredness and dementia complicates everything. Afterward it is so clear.

8/14/12

Speaking for Two

Yesterday we met with our lawyer, along with two financial advisors, in her office high above the Grand Rapids skyline. Sometimes we chat about family and such but not today. I sensed she had pressing business on her mind. She has known us for many years and seems to have a great memory for the details of our estate and the provisions in our will. We needed to discuss the changes our family—divorce and dementia, and how both would influence us financially and legally. In the last will we granted each other durable power of attorney, meaning either of us can sign legal papers for the other. It dawned on me what a huge step that represents for anyone in my situation. Now a copy of the document is always in my purse.

Before the meeting, I tried to prepare Fritz for the topics we would be covering and while driving to our appointment, repeated the list once more. Once again he had retained little of our talk, or of the family meeting we had with our advisors a month ago when the same things were discussed. I reviewed that the only reason we had to go to the lawyer was so that all our ideas would be covered legally.

During the meeting we got into complicated stuff like trusts and lifetime gift exemptions and executors. The back and forth by the professionals was swift and efficient. Many things were new. There was no time to slowly try to explain the technicalities. Soon, I sensed that Fritz was lost. Turning to him often, seeking to be assured of his affirmation even though he may not have understood all the details. At one point, talking about a new trust, the lawyer said, "Paid by Fritz and administered by Carol." That seemed to fall in-line with his long-standing joke about where the money came from, and it pleased him. Did he realize that I was being put in charge of all of "his" money?

The meeting ended amicably. We left with the two young advisors. Going down the elevator, Fritz began what has become his litany, the story of how he came by his funds. He remains in awe of a long ago decision of a drug company to patent his scientific discovery, against his advice. Many years later other drug companies were using the mechanism in drug productions, and Fritz was informed of royalties coming his way. It is a good story, but best if it is the first time one hears it. For the two advisors, this may have been the twentieth time.

They are kind, respectful and professional and never let on that it is old information. I wonder now how long ago they suspected Fritz's dementia based on that repeated story. When I finally told them confidentially about the diagnosis, it may have felt like old news. For the last year I have been communicating to them without copying Fritz, after I realized how confusing it was becoming. Fritz would print emails, try to keep track of them and ask me to fill in the background. Now I verbally review before and after meetings just for the record. My written summaries and letters caused greater confusion or were simply not read.

The meeting made me aware we had crossed into new territory. Not only was I remembering for two, now I was also speaking for two. Throughout our long marriage I have tried never to speak for him or let him speak for me. As in-

Tired from a mountain climb

agreement we have always been on major topics, neither of us would dare to say, "Fritz thinks that _____ or Carol thinks that _____." He was always there to speak for himself and he knew better than to speak for me.

About a year ago we met someone new in a university development office. The man looked askance when I answered his questions while Fritz was right there. Although it was necessary, it didn't feel right. We were talking about giving a grant to the institution and my speaking for Fritz appeared unseemly, like that of a pushy wife. I have tried letting Fritz explain while quietly supplying the fact or word that he cannot find. That works only in non-technical discussions.

Suddenly I have become "our" voice. The responsibility feels heavy: reflecting his wishes and opinions, sorting out shared beliefs and figuring out if what he says is genuine or influenced by his dementia. Once a supremely generous man, he now questions gifts and expenditures. It is an unsettling example of what the former Fritz would not do. Enticed by the offer of discounts, he opened two new credit cards. When I pay for something for our kids, he thinks they should pay their own way. When we eat out, he complains either about the price or the food. On the other hand, when someone helps us at home, he is so thankful he'd pay twice the amount agreed upon.

When I attended a caregivers support group they offered little cards that read, "My companion has memory loss, please be patient." Mine might read, "My husband would like me to speak for him." Or "My husband has requested that I speak on his behalf." Or, "I'm not being a pushy broad, he has Alzheimer's."

I may be speaking for two but that will never be my choice.

8/22/12

End of Summer Assessment — Where are we now?

One day soon he will ask, do you think I am getting worse? I need to be ready with an answer. Fritz has not asked for a while, but has stated his assessment when he is at his lowest. The waters of clarity are always muddied because of two types of wellness, mental and physical. When he is tired he is sure he will never get well, or he dreams of the magical year since radiation when a doctor said the effects could be gone. Often, when physically tired, his mental powers are overwhelmed by fatigue. He cannot think straight, he says. His desk and papers becomes a jumble of voices calling out to him but not making sense.

It is now August, near the end of the summer. He learned of the cancerous tumor in his cheek last November that was quickly removed in December. Early 2012 we spent going to radiation treatments, from which he has been recovering ever since. In May on a routine check-up with the neurologist, he recommended an increased dosage of Fritz's meds for stabilizing his Alzheimer's disease. That decision was based on the doctor's exam and conversation with Fritz and with me. The doctor concluded he was getting worse.

Knowing him better than anyone, it has never occurred to me to overlook or deny the changes that I see, but it is sometimes difficult to note them. The changes in Fritz happen slowly and vary by the time of day or the day of the week. There is nothing static. Fritz often tries harder when we are with friends; some do not notice the signs of memory loss. Old age looks much the same or creates an expectation that someone of his age could easily be slipping. Sometimes it is our children or people we meet with periodically who can note the changes better than I.

We have the car radio set for NPR so most of our long drives produce lots of interesting but unrelated information. Usually one news story depends on the listeners' memory of previous stories on the same topic. When making a comment or talking back to the radio about a controversial news item, I realize he is not listening. Now he has taken to declaring, "I am not interested in that," and switching off the radio or saying "there has to be something else." It is futile—his disinterest is broad.

For a long time, I have realized that incidental learning has all but disappeared. All the little clues one gets from a snippet of this or sight of that or a casual conversation

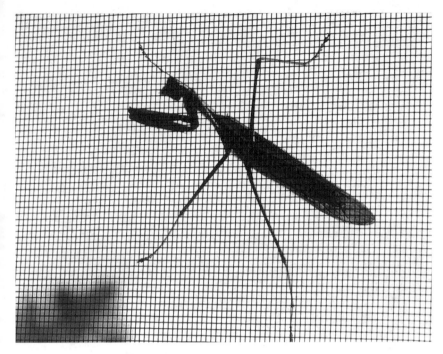

Praying Mantis on door screen

are gone. Things like the price of gas—he has no interest in comparison or change, probably because he cannot remember how much it was.

Some powers of notice have increased. For the first time in so long, he is looking at the clouds and constantly amazed. He comments endlessly from his passenger seat about the abundance or lack of green in the environment. He has taken to noticing the swan family on our lake every day. This is the time the young ones must learn to fly so they can leave "home." Several times Fritz has called their antics to my attention. The parents teach the children to fly but it is a long road of trial and error. It is fun to watch if you have the time and patience. Today he spotted a praying mantis on

Tori and Grandpa hunting for Wildflowers in Lead King

our screen door. We watched, photographed and speculated about why he was not leaving the screen. We then sat on the deck for a long time. I can't remember the last time we did that—in the morning.

He even took out his camera yesterday and wandered around taking shots of the garden abundance as well some lingering wildflowers. Pictures are carefully exposed, framed and all the subjects are in focus. He notices even moving things, often spotting small, scurrying critters. He thinks his years of hunting small game increased those powers. I am thankful he still has them.

Probably one of the biggest changes is with television. He used to enjoy it as a diversion, while I was concerned that he used it as his default mode. We watch a lot of news. He routinely turns to me in the middle of a story and says, "What is that all that about?" Of course a news story unfolds and if you try to explain something midstream you miss the next thoughts and often the summary. If we mute the sound for explanation, we miss the next item. We do record the shows, but most often watch in real time. During this heavily political season, the news is peppered with interest for me. It is way too much for him. Compared to four years ago—there is a huge change. Compared to three months ago—more change, but harder to document.

But what will I say when he asks the "do you think" question? First we'll put it back to him—do you sense you are getting worse? He will concentrate on the physical at first but I will try to move him toward the mental status. Depending on the day and how he feels, he might say that the medications have helped a lot—"don't you think?" I will agree but know at other times his assessment and my own might be different. If I say, yes you are getting worse, what will that do to his spirit? Where do honesty and prudence meet? My role as encourager is more important. I'll conclude with my latest mantra, "Just do the best with what you have."

That is all any of us can do. We cannot live in a past generation or in our former prime of life. Even without dementia or physical assaults, we will always change with age. To be at peace with that is difficult for one who was always on the "cutting edge." He is now being undermined at every turn, not in that gradual decline that comes with age but with sharp downs and a few temporary ups. At times we grieve our losses; at times we just carry on, adjusting as best we can to a reality of "getting worse."

One of the saddest things about this decline is his self-assessment. He often calls himself a "dummy" or an "idiot" for doing things that led him in the wrong direction. I beg him not to use those words of blame and guilt. I want to shout, *"You are brilliant but your cursed disease will no longer let it show."* Some diseases you can fight and feel good that you have not let them get the better of you. Alzheimer's is like a rock wall that gets thicker and thicker, taller and taller. There is no way around, through or over. Maybe I will find a little chink in the wall; I might leave a note for God. "Give us the grace to be content on this side of this immoveable wall."

8/23/12

Staying Positive

We all try to do it. Stay Up so life does not get us Down. On particularly glum days we grasp at straws of light just to keep going, knowing so well what the alternative might be: depression, stagnation, plodding through the day with joyless movement. Sometimes one of my children will report about their "terrible, awful day," but always after the worst is over and there is some sense that he or she prevailed. The words or the sounds I hear convey triumph.

So when their dad seems to be slipping down one of the kids throws a little lifeline. Yesterday, when he was particularly tired after church, Doug tried to get off the failure mode and on to a winning track. "Can you think of a couple of things that make you feel happy today?" he asked, as he might ask a child he counsels at school. It was a good try but the negative workout track just kept Fritz's mind returning to his own failure. "I can't remember a word from the sermon, even though it brought tears to my eyes more than once." "I never had self-confidence and now it is getting worse."

I brought along a soda for him to drink right after church. We have all noticed much more negativity when he is tired or hungry. He looked at it for a while until we pressed him to take a drink. He sipped slowly while we hoped for a mega dose of caffeine and sugar to buoy his spirits. Twenty minutes later he was still on the same circular track. I left them in the van to get some carryout lunch and returned to see Doug was still trying to catch up to him with a little hope. Doug offered his own answer to his question. "I'll tell you what brings me joy today: going to church with you and Mom and having time to talk together." Then on the more practical level, "I know it is a long trip to my house for you to pick me up. I'll ask my friends if they would mind transporting me, to save you the trip. That way we could meet there and still sit together." Doug was so clear and so logical. But the mind that took in the information was muddied and unable to jump from problem to solution. We will go to plan B next Sunday, even though it will mean a loss of time together for all of us. Doug and I know that even these family experiences may be in the countdown phase.

We ate our lunch together in the pleasant atmosphere of Doug's home. Calm, unhurried and hunger satisfied. Some mutual friends stopped by and we laughed and talked. Fritz seemed to enjoy himself. But on the way home he was all gloom. I suggested he sleep on the long drive; he insisted he could not. About fifteen minutes before home he fell asleep and when we walked in the door he went directly to the bed. I tried to wake him up in forty-five minutes but he continued sleeping. I finally woke him and said he might confuse night and day if he slept longer. He used to worry about naps ruining his night sleep, but that never happens any more. Sleep is a wonderful escape from his treadmill of a mind.

Naps usually leave him refreshed for a while. Food does the same thing—like a little gas for a motor riding on fumes. But more sleep like the eight plus hours he gets every night, does not result in more energy, but less. The tiredness begins again; the complaining begins again. Something different hurts every morning. Taking a shower wipes him out. He eats the same oatmeal breakfast he has for forty years but not with the same bodily effect. Coffee gets his mind going but only for a short while—which he tries to capitalize on at his desk.

Fritz has an analytical brain—he is always evaluating and comparing—a trait which made him a successful scientist. He is creative. He often led his research group of students and post-docs in a quest for the unknown, a search that sought answers using the painfully slow process of bench research. In the world of competitive grants application, he had to map out the work of the group for five years once he got their corroboration and make a convincing case for their plan. He was never without good funding. Even when he chose to retire, he had just been given a lifetime chair in the department and had two more years on a grant.

His old instincts are still there but today's mind defies order as well as creative discovery. I have been offering to sit with him so we can find some order in the chaos of his papers and files. Thanks to sticky notes, he has layers upon layers of lists attached to each other. He fears he will miss something if he throws anything away because his brain no longer remembers incidental things. When he makes a new list, the fact that he wrote a similar note yesterday is not apparent. I urged him to write his lists in a small spiral note pad which he could consult every day. Then if something is done he can cross it off. Way too logical!

But the most confounding thing to me is to sit in his desk chair and consider his former order; file folders neatly marked and grouped by categories in his pullout desk cabinet and horizontal files along the wall. A few years ago, our granddaughter put category labels on the outside so they would be easy to find. Every purchase, every home repair, every important contact—all recorded for future reference. There is just one problem: he can no longer locate the zone or the file he needs. A paper that should be filed does not make it off a pile on his desk. Or he sometimes puts the wrong piece of paper in a folder and loses it forever. His system is gone leaving no past or future reference for him.

His most active category is now: Doctors. His pattern has been to write notes about each visit and file them and record upcoming appointments on his calendar. Now he forgets by the time we get home. Without papers, he worries about what to tell each doctor we consult and wants to "sit down and talk about it before the visit." After we do, I make a list, but don't need it after so much review. He never looks at the list. I keep all the post-visit papers now and occasionally it unnerves him not to have notes of what happened last time. When I tell him, he says, "I never heard that."

Analytical, organized, finding creative solutions to complex problems—those were his strengths. This disease is cruel—taking his most reliable traits and throwing them to the four winds. Of course it is hard to name a joyous moment when his son asks. Pleasure is as fleeting as papers left in stacks. He can only see the one on top and that one needs attention. Add it to the worry list.

When we are in bed and have turned off the lights, I try to name the little joys of the day. He agrees with each one. I rub his back until he falls asleep, hopefully thinking about the good of the day. Tomorrow we will search again for a little happiness.

9/17/12

Planning a Color Tour

Early October and we bask in the most beautiful fall in recent years. Golden and burnt orange mingled with this year's lingering green. Sugar maple red behind rusty Indian grass alongside the swale. New England asters of purple next to the tiny white and pale blue kind, accent the driveway. All the weather unpredictability of this spring and summer is outweighed by a gorgeous, traditional Michigan fall.

Fritz talks of taking a color tour even though every drive to town gives us the tour of our lives. He can't seem to get enough of the startling sights all around us. He is too weak to walk the short distance to the woods and photograph what he sees. Yesterday he and son-in-law Dave drove the newly tuned golf cart and took a mini-color tour into the woods near our house. Fritz didn't have his camera so we may want to return later. Making the walk without him and taking a few pictures, I see that his "artist's eye" makes all the difference in getting a good shot. After downloading the photos, it is easy to divide them by amateur and artist. He has tried to teach me about lighting and plane and composition. Being more of a point and shoot kind of photographer, I never know what the shot will look like until I can examine it on the computer screen.

Why does this year's show impress me so? Why can't Fritz get enough of it? I think we fear the end. Not the end of the season and the beginning of drab. Not the signal that gardening time is almost over. We fear the end of enjoyment. We fear the end of his life. His health is precarious and his prospects limited. Tomorrow we will learn the results of tests of blood and bone.

The real color tour is planned for Friday. Daughter Barb has offered to be the tour guide while I am at a meeting. This is something she wants to do with her dad. We are all hanging on to special things. First we need to get past the family meeting the doctor suggested would be appropriate when she tells what she knows. We all know that is an ominous sign. His loss of strength and energy has been profound—we are looking for a name for what ails him. We are looking for a way forward.

What we don't know is whether the Michigan color will still be as vibrant and beautiful once we learn the news. I had a bit of a clue today driving home from a short meeting downtown. The colors never looked more intense, with an overcast sky and rain glistening on the leaves. Trees we passed yesterday are redder and fuller. The wild grape vines drape the trees with yellow stoles. As I "oohed and awed" I turned to Fritz. His head drooped; he didn't look out the window. He has always been tuned into the weather. Like a farmer it dictates his decisions. I think his second sense already knows the weather ahead does not look good.

God knows our souls need the color and sunshine and a good harvest. Each day of summer God's blessings were more than we imagined possible. Divine care surrounds even the unpredictable winds and waves. I am relying on God's care to see us through any storm—even the one forecast for tomorrow.

10/3/12

Tiredness Has a Name

On the way to the doctor's appointment I mentally reviewed the sudden sequence of events that got us to this place. Several weeks ago, when Fritz expressed concern over a lump he felt in his abdomen, I almost dismissed it. There had been so many complaints about bodily ills that flared but then disappeared so I learned to wait before calling the doctor with false alarms. He mentioned the odd bulge but it was several days before I felt it while he was still in bed. Fritz knew this was not normal and speculated it might be his spleen. I pulled out the anatomy book.

Fritz's internist agreed to see us right away. We realized his concern when he sent us immediately to have a scan. The ultrasound tech audibly gasped before labeling it: "large spleen." The tiny, rarely mentioned organ, except if ruptured in an accident, was three to four times its usual size. Next stop a Hematologist consult.

Dr. Polavaram, who was relatively new to the area, had the earliest opening at the Greenville office near us. We entered the large, gleaming exam room, where a small woman with dark eyes and an East Indian accent, welcomed us. She did not ask Fritz to lie down to be examined; she wanted to talk face to face. Soon he was telling his life story, including the parts about being a professor of Molecular Biology and about restoring a prairie on our land after retirement. She wanted to know the man who had the disease; learning about the disease could come later. Her voice soothed a worried man.

She sent us across the parking lot to the hospital lab for blood tests. The lab tech appeared shocked by the long list, but soon began to draw fourteen vials, while telling someone to run for orange juice. I pushed the woozy man to our car and helped him in. The doctor also ordered a bone marrow biopsy the next day at a hospital in Grand Rapids, where the she also had an office.

He still complained of tiredness the next day as we drove to town. I called ahead to make sure that I could bring him to the front door. I nearly panicked when the woman at the front desk said she thought the office was on the other side of the building but we could follow the hall to get there. He refused a wheelchair. I was desperate to find the right place quickly but it was not to be. A person in a non-medical office called to get directions and we retraced out steps, only to find the right place very near the entrance. We fell into seats and waited. I was too exhausted and stressed to complain.

We entered another smaller sterile exam room—brightened only by the doctor's gentle hands and soothing voice. Fritz bravely accepted the painful poke by a large needle into his hipbone.

Doctor Polavaram called me the next evening—with the news that the situation did not look good. I asked as many questions as my numb mind would allow. She never hurried me. At her suggestion, I agreed to take several of our adult children to the appointment the next day.

I pondered the news all-night—alone. I wanted the doctor to tell us everything at the same time. She would be able to answer our questions. Again we entered the same exam room, a group of four now, with plenty of room for Doug's wheelchair. The exam table remained untouched. We talked—Dr. Polavaram letting Fritz take the lead. She seemed to know that Fritz perceived the news before she spoke it: cancer, aggressive, untreatable—Mantle Cell Lymphoma. Her heart seemed to be breaking along with each of ours.

A starry, starry night

Daughter Barb asked the all-important question: how long does he have? Even though the news of cancer did not shock us, the timeline did: "weeks to months." We talked some more and one of us mentioned Rituxan and the part Fritz's discovery played in the development of that drug. The irony was not lost on any of us; the miracle drug could not help him.

As I stumbled out of the exam room, carrying the weight of "terminal," the doctor said, "You might want to begin Hospice right away." She had delivered bad news, now she offered something I already knew was good. Just like that we were ushered into end-of-life care. We slowly walked to our cars. Around us sunshine and bold color belied our sad hearts.

10/15/12

Let Evening Come

By Jane Kenyon

Let the light of late afternoon
shine through chinks in the barn, moving
up the bales as the sun moves down.

Let the cricket take up chafing
as a woman takes up her needles
and her yarn. Let evening come.

Let dew collect on the hoe abandoned
in long grass. Let the stars appear
and the moon disclose her silver horn.

Let the fox go back to its sandy den.
Let the wind die down. Let the shed
go black inside. Let evening come.

To the bottle in the ditch, to the scoop
in the oats, to air in the lung
let evening come.

Let it come, as it will, and don't
be afraid. God does not leave us
comfortless, so let evening come.

TODAY

Jake on Flat Iron dock

CHAPTER ONE

SUNDOWN

Reflection

My good friend worked as a hospice nurse for many years before retiring. Together we wrote an article about the value of hospice care for our church's denominational magazine. I came away from our planning sessions convinced that if I were dying I'd want hospice care to see me through. The same gentle spirit she showed to her patients, reached past any previous reservations and gave me a new perspective on "a good death." She expressed deep sadness when people who were dying refused hospice until their last days.

Three of the hospice team visited right away, the nurse, the social worker and the spiritual counselor. I quickly learned about their services, made visit schedules and signed papers. A copy of the most important paper was left with me—the Do Not Resuscitate Order. If Fritz had a medical emergency and had to be transported to the hospital, I could use the DNR to guide the personnel. Without the order, they would do everything possible to revive him, even if it increased his suffering.

The good people from hospice gave us enormous comfort on our journey. Amie "our" nurse came every week, whether her technical nursing skills were needed or not. She got to know us well and moved in tandem with our rhythms, scheduling her visits at Fritz's best times of day. The doctor came less frequently, not to treat but to fully understand our wishes and

okay any changes in pain medications. The others called less
often because we had plenty of family support and our pastor
came frequently. A volunteer, about Fritz's age, came several
times to keep him company. When we needed help in the
evening, a male nurse came out. Then there was Cassie, an
aide, who gently helped Fritz shower and later bathe in bed.
He was leery at first, but she brought such cheer, he could not
resist. The large hospice sticker stayed right by the phone—a
nurse was just a phone call away. Always available, always
helpful—they reduced our stress greatly.

Palliative care promotes care instead of cure. There comes
a time in every life when death is inevitable. I will be forever
thankful that we could make peace with death with hospice by
our side. Another of God's graces.

Dementia Trumped by Disease

There was a time…

when Alzheimer's was king of my thoughts—Alzheimer's,
the disease with the crazy name, which no one could
diagnose until after death. Why didn't it have a more user-
friendly sound to it like Palmer's or Morton's? When I used
the more generic term dementia, friends wondered if I didn't
want people to know that Fritz had the disease, so laden with
stigma. I used dementia because of its softer sound. It did not
seem to evoke the same mental picture even though it mean't
the same thing. But just mention the "A" word and strangers
teared up and guests changed the subject.

There was a time…

when I read all the books, searched out online information
and desperately looked for other women walking in a similar

space. A support group from the Alzheimer's Association became a haven but weighed me down with more information than I could handle and a heavy reference book in case the leaders forgot something. I learned that "If you know one person with Alzheimer's, you know one person with Alzheimer's." I watched those disturbing videos of people in various stages. Yes, I knew only one—the man I walked alongside.

There was a time…

when I speculated what his decline might look like. Would his behavior continue to inch up slightly and then ever so gradually slide down? Or would there be a sudden loss of recognition or an inability to do basic things like brushing his teeth? The books conjured up some pretty frightening pictures. My friends and I shared notes and it was clear that there was no pattern. One talked about her husband losing an inch a week. One man could fluently speak the language he had taught even as his English diminished.

There was a time…

when I worried over when to insist that Fritz could no longer drive. I even sent for copies of a pamphlet specific for Alzheimer's and driving because I thought our family would need to convince him not to drive, when he thought he could. Those pamphlets came the other day and I realized how much had changed in a mere four weeks. Now he is too tired to drive.

There was a time…

when I wrote essays each time I felt a change in our relationship because of dementia. I wrote many short pieces, which helped sort things and might, I thought, someday help others in my situation. In one, I contrasted Fritz's slow dying to that of a friend with advanced cancer.

...Now is the time to live a different story. Fritz is dying swiftly. Alzheimer's is no longer king. My mind can hardly assimilate the strange alterations this news forces upon me. When we got the news, we could only speculate how long he has to live. We prepare for the worst case: weeks.

The pain I anticipate, of making difficult end-of-life decisions, disappears. Treatment is not possible: neither of us have to refuse.

We wait for whatever is in store. The final road will surely be complicated because of the combination of dementia and cancer. We pray for dignity in dying. We even pray that this last leg of his journey will be short and smooth. The anguish Fritz feels about his slow loss of mental powers is replaced by the slow letting go of life itself.

Fritz tells me he is ready to die and unafraid. Suddenly, I am less ready and more afraid. Oh, God, please give us both "strength for today and bright hope for tomorrow..."

11/4/12

Last Wishes

"What would you like to do in the time you have left?" a hospice worker asked on her first visit to our home. It was also the question we asked each other when we left the doctor's office after getting the diagnosis. First thoughts included going to Marble one last time, going to northern Michigan to see the fall colors and making sure the garden was ready for winter. We soon admitted that fifty years of memories in that little mountain village would have to take the place of an actual trip. I have often said that just closing our eyes and saying the word can bring us back to that beloved place.

Trips of any kind, especially involving an overnight stay, were also ruled out just because of his lack of stamina and confusion in a strange place. The day of the diagnosis was as glorious a fall day as any we have experienced. We drank in the color. Even our own acreage offered more than we could take in: the maroon sumac, the deep crimson dogwood, and the golden leaves of the redbud tree. Fritz did take the color-tour ride with our daughter, Barb, driving an hour north and back. But they came home concluding that our own Hart Street with its mighty trees, overhung with golden grape leaves was the most beautiful sight they had seen.

As for the garden, this entire growing season Fritz had garden help from a young man from Kenya. Fritz could rest easy today as he watched from the kitchen window. From this vantage point, he had a wonderful sense of peace that Leonard knew the garden ropes and would carry on when he was gone. His beloved asparagus and raspberries, and an abundance of carrots and winter squash were in good hands. As soon as harvest was over, the soil would be prepared for next year. A wish fulfilled. Fritz hoped that Leonard would also raise enough food for his family next year.

One chore, not a last wish but a duty, was to tell Fritz's friends and associates that he was dying. This was not something we wanted to do but the alternative was letting them know after the fact. We decided that while he still felt well enough to enjoy talking to people we would ask close friends to come by, during his best times of day. His dearest friends would be the saddest to meet but also the most desired companions.

He immediately thought of the friends who had come to be known as "the gang." Six couples who, ever since high school or college have been our most loyal friends, For about ten years after graduation we went our own ways—grad school, jobs, and kids. Without warning there seemed to be a collective "missing" which led us to reunite at least once a year, even though several of us lived far away. We found something in each other that was irreplaceable. Love and respect, shared values and dreams, and our faith all rolled into a lasting friendship.

Years passed. After we all retired from our first careers and lived closer, our gatherings became more frequent. We found a good restaurant with a private room where we could sit at tables facing each other and really talk. Last year Fritz held back from telling them about his Alzheimer's diagnosis, focusing on other losses instead.

As we aged we seemed to share wisdom more than events. Within the group we have faced our share of serious illnesses, divorces of children, disappointments, but we always found lots to be thankful for. Several years ago, after one man had a sudden heart attack and another had his third bout with cancer, we talked about a time when one of us would be missing from around the table. I may have been the one to suggest: "Even if a spouse dies we should pledge to always include the other in our gatherings."

Little did I know Fritz would be the first to face certain death. How do you say goodbye to your best friends, each one dear in their own way? Fritz admitted that it would be painful and emotionally exhausting to have six separate visits. Then came another of those last wishes while he still had time: "I'd like to have them all come here together!"

The group already had a date on the books for a "gang" dinner. After telling them the news about Fritz's aggressive

First Calvin swim team — 1958

lymphoma and "weeks to months" prognosis, we suggested that they come to our house before going to the restaurant. A dinner, which might include us, even catered here, was out of the question. We made plans for a final gathering. They offered to come earlier if Fritz's health deteriorated. But it held, at least enough for him to greet his best friends from his living room chair.

And thus, we became part of a "group hug" like none other we have known in our lives. Before they came, Fritz was nervous. From his perch he wanted to see that everything was in order. The magazines straightened with the most appropriate on top; one tiny finger print on the glass coffee table removed; the chairs arranged so all fourteen of us

College fun with the "gang."

could sit in one big circle. As with many things those days I had moved from scoffing at superficial details to arranging everything just to make him comfortable. His real concerns he could not express. Could all of us put aside the sadness of our coming separation long enough to hang onto the way things always were between us?

I tried to put myself in their shoes—coming to see a friend perhaps for the last time. If it had been me I would have worried about the awkward moments, saying the right things, or breaking into tears. When they drove up to the house, one by one, it was like a funeral procession except that all the cars were white and didn't have those little flags on the top. Welcoming them, some gave extra long hugs and asked me in hushed tones, "How are *you* doing?" I directed them into the living room where they greeted Fritz, smiling from his seated position. The gathering began with the same banter we had always known together; all fear melted in the glow of our vintage friendship.

Fritz was himself but a little less reserved, as the gang insisted he have the floor more often. They told their old stories and lived in the glow of good days long gone. We all marveled at our lasting bond of togetherness. They wanted to know about the history of his illness but most of all how he was coping with the daily weakness that cancer imposed on his body. Surely there was collective relief that he was not in pain. And perhaps the lasting impression—he was not afraid.

The preacher in the group suggested a prayer to end our time together. He volunteered to lead us even while admitting, "I'm a pretty emotional guy." And so we prayed, holding hands tightly letting tears come. In those moments we knew our shared faith was tested—by the ultimate enemy, death. How did a life with Christ yield to death in Christ? Could we contemplate eternal life for Fritz, even as we grieved?

Our group hug was wide, with deep love running from hand to hand around the circle. The friends lingered only long enough to give goodbye hugs to Fritz and me. I watched the white cars roll out of the driveway, moving on, as life must. Alone again, lingering tears came as we pondered the gift of enduring friendship and ties that could not be broken, even by death.

For Fritz, one wish fulfilled; one man at peace.

10/28/12

Lord of All Hopefulness

Lord of all hopefulness, Lord of all joy,
whose trust, ever childlike, no cares could destroy,
be there at our waking, and give us, we pray,
your bliss in our hearts, Lord, at the break of the day.

Lord of all eagerness, Lord of all faith,
whose strong hands were skilled at the plane and the lathe,
be there at our labors, and give us, we pray,
your strength in our hearts, Lord, at the noon of the day.

Lord of all kindliness, Lord of all grace,
your hands swift to welcome, your arms to embrace,
be there at our homing, and give us, we pray,
your love in our hearts, Lord, at the eve of the day.

Lord of all gentleness, Lord of all calm,
whose voice is contentment, whose presence is balm,
be there at our sleeping, and give us, we pray,
your peace in our hearts, Lord, at the end of the day.

Lord, Come

It had been five weeks since we got the news of Fritz's lymphoma. First came the relief when a name was given to the ill that kept him sidelined and weak for months. He did not gain strength when the radiation treatments ended. Now we knew why. Giving it a name gave us something, although not the something we hoped for.

We also felt relief that he did not have to endure a long, slow deconstruction by dementia. It was a bright thought, though not one easily put into words. We had to talk about death now, the final destruction of his body. He worried over the unfairness of it all, not for himself—for me—always for me.

The doctor said the cancer could go quickly and wanted us to be ready. The cancer advanced stealthily through his body, showing itself occasionally with a sudden sore or bruise. When he spoke of an ache or pain there was a pause before calling the hospice nurse, while we determined if it was a passing discomfort. The aches came and went. A hospice nurse warned me his situation could change suddenly. She left a box of meds in the fridge to be used, at her instruction, when warranted. These days the gradual decline in physical strength was less pronounced than his mental confusion.

He could not remember events for more than a day or two. He turned to me often when trying to tell someone about the diagnosis, saying, "Carol can tell this better than I can." I felt like the medical historian of one.

Some folks get the terminal diagnosis and create the "still want to do," list. But reality set in as we walked slowly out of the doctor's office that day toward the car. He showed his weakness even on that short walk. His desire to go anywhere ended soon after that. Even the little color tour by car in glorious mid-October left him exhausted.

We are here for the duration. We do not know if the end is in sight. When the hospice nurse mentions, "we can always re-certify Fritz if it goes beyond six months," the thought gives me pause. Can either of us hang on in this limbo state? How long will this slow and labored life continue? Can I find the patience and peace going forward I had in the early days? What will impatience look like in me? I cannot not imagine that it will be noble or pretty.

Pleasures for Fritz are few: reading in short spurts; visitors who come but don't stay too long; television if the topics are not too complicated or controversial; and, watching some World War II videos. Perhaps his biggest joys are visits from children or just the two of us being together. We certainly find time to talk even though I feel the need to keep our conversations uncomplicated. If we delve too deeply into a troubling topic near bedtime, he dwells on the sadness and regrets far into the night. With no way to process them, he finally falls into a troubled sleep. I cannot voice my concerns, because he finds it upsetting that I might be conflicted in any way. Putting on a steady façade, I often snuggle beside him in bed, troubled but silent.

What can we do with the time between now and death? Those empty spaces when there is nothing to look forward to? Facing today's void makes me wonder about living alone. I don't know what I'd do with an hour to myself, having forgotten how to plan for only one. Following Fritz's cues when he cannot explain them, I anticipated what he needs. I have no clue what I need.

Idzerd Van Dellen, an elderly pastor at a Denver church of my youth, ended his sermons with these words: "Come Lord Jesus, come quickly!" In the earthly sense, it seems cheap and callous for me to say that now—because I wish for haste, not for myself but for Fritz. I continue praying for mercy so he does not have to suffer, longing for the Spirit's presence, and stating my solemn request for Fritz's release from pain. I want his days to be peaceful, just as the end of all days on earth will be for him. So come, Lord.

11/11/12

The Last Holiday

I didn't expect Fritz to last until Thanksgiving. The journey from weak to weaker continued even though he tried to carry on. He shaved and showered every day, got dressed and often went to his desk in the basement, hand over hand holding onto the rail. He wanted to get his papers in order. Soon, the basement time became frustrating, as he was too tired to think and just wanted to lie down. Coming up the stairs was hard work. We tried to find things to do in the living room. He finally finished the book he'd been plowing through. He didn't want to begin another.

When Thanksgiving was two weeks away it was time to decide if our tentative plan to gather as a family would work. Fritz's morning routine had slowed to a point that a shower took every smidgeon of his morning energy and often left him ready to nap. Mid-afternoon after a two-hour nap had been his best time of day, so we decided to eat about three so he could join us at the table.

Many times during the week I doubted that the plan had any chance of succeeding. Wake-up time after a nap was taking longer, so we could not really count on timing. Lots of "ifs"—in the end we just had to go for it. I was to handle their dad's schedule at home and the two girls divided up the food to bring, freeing me to control the morning schedule without cooking. In the end I couldn't shake decades of having fun and loving the holiday rush of baking pies and squash and adding other touches to the appetizer buffet.

All the while I kept my eye on the clock, planning to make Fritz a small lunch and scuttle him off to bed. It worked and the bedroom door was closed before the first cooks arrived, one with a half-baked turkey in tow. My kitchen has a double

Family at Christmas watching Chris's video

oven just for occasions like this and soon both filled for cooking or warming. I warned the grandkids to hold down the noise but exuberance is just part of any holiday at their grandparent's house.

What will be—was. Grandpa got up a little earlier than planned because he didn't want to miss the fun. He hobbled with his walker to his black chair, quickly evacuated by a long legged grandson. His eyes shown with something like glee. As long as he didn't have to stand or walk he was fine. Finally, the food was all laid out on the sideboard buffet, and twelve holiday hungry people filled their plates. Grandpa moved to the kitchen and ate a nice little sampler plate as he sat at the head of the long table, with his family all around.

In late afternoon we all went outside for a family picture. Our two sons-in-law walked Fritz outside where the tripod and camera were waiting. We knew he didn't have stamina for a long wait. He draped his arm around my shoulders, not so much as a loving gesture but as a prop. We made it though the photo op just in time to help Fritz back inside to his familiar black chair.

From that vantage point he watched old video productions— strange conglomerates of various home videos and one from his brother's Super 8, a shaky hodge-podge of film. All were great for the memories they brought back. Several kids saw moving pictures of their parents as children for the first time.

Grandpa held up so the crowd stayed on. Dessert was an outrageous number of the best pies in the world. Our stomachs were too full, but no one complained.

As the last vehicle left the drive, I looked at Fritz. He was still happy—no complaints. It had not been too much for him. The next day he was sure to pay the price, but today was more than he ever expected after hearing the "weeks to months" prognosis.

There was only one problem. Three of the grandchildren could not be with us on Thanksgiving Day. To get that one last, grand together time we decided to have a "left-over Sunday." A repeat performance worried me. This time I insisted on his early nap so we could accommodate the time-schedule of our oldest granddaughter who had to travel five hours back to school after eating. We also had our hearts set on another family picture with everyone present, this time in the house. With fifteen assembled around the big table, our son prayed words of thanks for all the blessings of the past and assurance that God would supply each of our needs.

Grandpa reading Dani's card

Fritz once again found enough strength to enjoy a great meal and good conversation.

As everyone prepared to leave, there were good-bye hugs and words of thanks. Each grandchild bent down to hug Grandpa before hurrying out to the car. How many had that tear in their eye that I had? How many thought, *"Is this the last holiday that Grandpa will enjoy?"* Holidays always string together in our minds—Thanksgiving always signals the advent of Christmas.

In the calm after they were gone, Fritz reflected on the wonderful days of the Thanksgiving season. Tired but joyful in his own way, Fritz had a sense of completeness. He couldn't ask for more. I told him that the kids offered to come back to trim the Christmas tree. He looked puzzled. A Christmas tree, Christmas—why? He seemed to say, "This is my final holiday." The grand finale.

Now, like old Simeon after he saw the Christ child, let this servant depart in peace. Seventy-five years of celebrating the birth of Christ, now it is time to see God face-to-face.

11/27/12

Alone Together

"Let there be spaces in your togetherness, and let the winds of the heavens dance between you. Love one another but make not a bond of love: Let it rather be a moving sea between the shores of your souls. Fill each other's cup but drink not from one cup. Give one another of your bread but eat not from the same loaf. Sing and dance together and be joyous, but let each one of you be alone, even as the strings of a lute are alone though they quiver with the same music."

—Khalil Gibran, *The Prophet*

Many years ago, a young couple I knew used this quote as their wedding vows. The words seemed odd at the time but have stuck with me ever since. Our marriage was built on togetherness and separation: those spaces "in our togetherness" that Khalil Gibran talked about in *The Prophet*. The spaces were always shorter than the times together, for practical reasons. For personal reasons the spaces were just as important. There were times of leaning and times of independence in our relationship—each of us knew that there must be a balance or one person might cripple the other. Driving, flying, leaving by some means seemed to refresh, not to destroy, the magnetic pull back home and being together.

During our most intense years of working, the time after all the kids were out of the house, we may have gotten the balance a little messed up. Two people can be more flexible than five about everything from meals to family vacations. There was no counterweight of people needing us at home to prevent overwork and overcommitment. About that time—especially for me—there was also questioning of satisfaction on the job and the relentless drive to meet other people's demands. My job was easier to leave; Fritz's not so much. I began creating my own writing business while he took on more leadership roles. The relentless responsibility took a toll. A bout with prostate cancer prompted him to offer his early retirement, and both of us gained a better perspective on life, leaving Cleveland for acreage in Michigan.

The first ten years of working for something other than pay, were intense years of exploration and creativity. He nurtured the earth on a large piece of land to fulfill a lifelong passion for growing things of beauty. He continued to garden for useful, edible vegetables and berries. He did not plant fruit trees as he had in the past; perhaps thinking that time was too short for their slow growth and eventual bearing of fruit. He ambitiously worked to restore a prairie on our land, with tall prairie grasses interspersed with many varieties of wildflowers. After years of waiting for them to take hold, he photographed them while I wrote about our life on the prairie.

Mercifully, the prostate cancer soon posed no threat. We continued our dance between togetherness and separation—between dependence and freedom. At least once a year, each of us traveled away from home without the other: I to writing classes in Iowa and he on hunting or fishing trips with friends. Each of us did some work for boards, which took us away from home. I taught some courses and he traveled to his previous workplace for a visiting committee of the medical school. We enjoyed the breaks from home and each other as well as the return. Together we went to Kenya and Uganda to help with the development work for a month each year.

Day-to-day, we spent times at home at two separate desks—mine on the second floor and his on the lower level. As if we still had jobs, we did the things we loved in solitude but always ate lunch and spent evenings together. In good weather we also worked together on the prairie and in the vegetable garden, although he was the prime mover for both. For all my feminist tendencies, we shared the necessary work around the house rather traditionally, he concentrating on the outside and the cars, and I the inside and the food.

The winds of heaven danced between us and God blessed our way of life. We had a lot to share during our togetherness. We were often fascinated and amazed that two so different people had managed to enrich the life of the other and stay married for so many years.

Togetherness brought its share of troubles. Communication is a delicate thing but over the years we could talk, and even though we have not always agreed, we could explain our cares and worries. We were good company for each other and enjoyed friends together. Little disputes arose, but thankfully in all the big things like politics, religion and values we were in lockstep. We argued fairly and listened to each other's point. My term "sparring partners" is an appropriate term for spouses like us that are high-spirited and occasionally confrontational. The kids wondered sometimes about com- patibility. In the end we found peace, not blissful peace, but a sense of "all-rightness."

We have entered in a new stage of togetherness. Beginning with signs of dementia about two years ago, his forgetfulness and inability to express himself are daily reminders. He cannot find the words he needs and often leaves me guessing about his meaning. The balance between two independent persons, who loved and also argued, is tilting. I have to be careful what I say—even a slight raise of the voice invites a full-blown argument. As his condition unevenly evolves, my responsibility is to understand his limitations. We can still converse but only about concrete not subtle matters. Slowly the identifiers in his speech are drifting away and only I can decipher where he is going with a story or request. We have become a new kind of team—though not of equals—he is clearly leaning on me. Sparring is a thing of the past.

It is difficult to live with a bright man, the one you have always depended on, as he becomes increasingly dependent on you. In addition to dementia, he carries the brunt of hurtful things: the cancerous tumor on his salivary gland, radiation, energy depletion and then a terminal diagnosis of lymphoma. This man who understands the mechanism of disease, now helpless in the larger medical treatment world. He cannot answer the most basic of questions: "Do you want something for pain? Have you had a bowel movement today?" He needs me to clarify; he needs me to remember.

On this last leg of our journey, Fritz remains at home with hospice care—not in a care center. We are tied together like never before. There are almost no spaces. Except for an occasional trip away for me, we are together. We are also alone. Fritz is alone in his journey toward death in the real world, no longer speculating but living into the end. Pain is real; death is the ultimate abstraction.

I ponder alone even while we are together—every day, all day.

12/2/12

The Dog and the Man

Two lasting pictures: a man walking slowly down the driveway to the barn; a dog walking slowly up the driveway to the house. Both are walking because it is their habit, not necessarily their present joy. The man rarely gets out these days. But by late afternoon feels he should try to make it to the barn; a short walk. He walks with uneven gait, planting his feet slightly apart with each step for stability. Once in the barn, he sits on his lawn mower until he finds the energy to move again. The trip back takes longer with stops to survey the prairie while he waits for strength to return. Although he has refused my company, I watch from the window in case he needs me. He enters the back door not with a smile of "I made it!" but only the blank look of a runner who finishes the race toward the end of the pack.

Jake, our black Labrador, who has been this man's constant companion, does not get out much anymore either. They do not look at each other and think, "Chase the Frisbee." The man is too weak to throw and the dog too weak to fetch. The old toy still covered with grit of former chases sits on the shelf.

Jake and I have had our pleasures too. Every morning for his dozen years, as soon as it was light, Jake and I would go out to feel the day. Hearing me open the pocket door to his room, he bounded up, hardly able to wait. Of course he had

Jake

other duties in mind but mostly it is just stretching those four legs on a brisk run down the driveway and then reluctantly going back inside for breakfast.

Now all walks are labored. The first barriers for Jake are the two steps from the back door to the floor of the garage. It is surprising that his skinny legs will hold him. He moves slowly. He no longer looks for an early morning snack of rabbit droppings. Only puddles near the barn draw his attention—he laps the cold water.

Both the man and the dog are wasting away with the same disease: lymphoma, a cancer of the white blood cells. For the man there was a long period of decline, mostly of energy and stamina. His strong body weakened. His arms and legs lost their girth. When I put my arms around him I feel only bones —no padding or toned muscles. We measure his strength by the length of his walk down the driveway. The garden he lovingly nurtured since early spring can only be admired from the kitchen window.

Fritz was the first to notice the large lump under Jake's jaw. I rushed him to the vet only to get the sad verdict. The vet could do nothing to change the course of the disease. I urged him to keep the dog alive at least as long as Fritz was expected to live. It worked for a while, but Jake's lymphoma moved quickly and Fritz's slowly. The dog often could not get up from the wooden kitchen floor without help. I could not lure him into the living room to sit by Fritz. Years of obedience to our wishes, kept him from lying on the carpet, which would have been an easier rising pad. Day after day he lay there almost motionless— Fritz a few feet away on his easy chair, unable to comfort the dog by his presence.

Finally we chose mercy over our desire to keep Jake alive. It was a difficult decision. Faithful dogs are a blessing. Dying dogs make us sad, for us and for them. Without language we don't know if they suffer. Jake could no longer do the things he loved—chasing a ball or a Frisbee, romping with kids, cleaning up my spills while cooking or chopping, waiting outside the garden fence for the man to toss him a vegetable or a berry. I could not bear the trip back to the vet so I asked our son-in-law to take Jake on his last ride.

We miss Jake every day, sometimes with a few tears and fond memories. Fritz is hopeful I can find companionship

Thanksgiving with family (minus Doug's kids)

in a dog when he can no longer be here for me. He often asks, "Do you think you will get another dog?" So much will change once I am alone; there is no answer.

Fritz cannot get out of his chair without assistance. He needs his walker for stability. He can no longer do the things that make him happy—puttering in the barn, a long walk, doing things with the grandkids, tilling the soil. He wishes for the mercy we humans can only accomplish with dogs—to be put out of his misery.

Someday the cancer will take him. It will not be soon enough for him. He was already dealing with dementia, dreading that slow decline into oblivion. We didn't choose cancer, but its appearance brought hope that his end would be shorter, more peaceful and dignified. Fritz is impatient with his cancer's slow progress. The winter is here; the garden and the abundant wildflowers have died. He wants to die too. He wants this painful parting over.

I pray for mercy for both of us. Spring always follows winter—a time for new life—here at our home on Flat Iron Lake or in a much better place. Come, Lord Jesus. Come quickly.

12/24/12

CHAPTER TWO

NIGHTFALL

The Waiting Game

Now that we are confined to home and have stopped most of our outside involvements, the days seem to be gone almost before they begin. They pass without highlights, without anticipation of things to come. I once wrote a meditation about the "elongated middle," the part we often forget when we relate events or high points of our lives. There are always the times between the times when almost nothing of note happens. I used the story of Noah and the ark as an example. Counting the number of days that Noah and crew were actually drifting in that big boat with no highlights—just a long, slow, monotonous drift.

I have a weekly ritual on Saturday night putting Fritz's medications in pill holders, one for morning and another for evening. Sunday-Saturday marked on the lids. There is also the daily ritual of making sure he takes the pills—fourteen in the morning, ten in the evening. Nothing emphasizes the regularity of the drifting days, as does this repetitious act. The days are passing relentlessly.

Part of the ritual requires planning ahead so each type of medicine does not run out. If the bottle contents are running low after being expended into the pill-holders, I have a week to order more. I remember so well, when we first got the diagnosis of "weeks to months," I wondered if I should order those meds that have three-month refills. Their use seemed improbable. No more. We are going on three months with no land in sight, like Noah waiting for the water to recede.

Some would think me heartless to write of our waiting time in this way. I have talked to survivors of their spouse's cancer, who say things like, "the doctor said three months and we got a year!" I have to think that their circumstances were different. I have to think that many parts of that extra bonus of time were marked by meaningful interactions and sharing some "hopes and fears of all the years." Reflection often marks endings or beginnings, like New Year's Eve tomorrow. Alzheimer's has robbed Fritz of that gift of looking backward with satisfaction and forward ready to claim God's promises. He can look way back with some clarity, but difficulty in finding words that he wants to use, has limited the sharing of events. I am one of the few who can slip words in which make the story complete. Time, place, specifics get lost in the mental jumble.

Most of the time he is stuck in the present, which stretches out each day with little to mark it. When others come over to brighten his day and give me some relief, he does not reflect on it once it is over. That absent short-term memory takes away even wonderful recent events, like Thanksgiving and Christmas celebrations with family. Many times he faults me for not telling him what is planned for a day. All would be fine if only he knew, he thinks.

I have stopped looking ahead. At first I thought about unfinished business and making plans for the end. Now, we muddle through these days together. I am resting on the promises and hopes of a better life after death for him. He is

Watching Chris' video

just resting. I know he has a deep-seated assurance of God's faithfulness even though right now the distant shoreline seems hazy. We are waiting because it is the only game playing in our household. Everyday I ask for God's grace to wait patiently and to help Fritz get to the other shore.

12/30/12

One Hour of One Day of Each Week

The days slog along; one following the other as if they did not know there was evening and morning of each. One long string of hours just runs together. Even sleep does not mark day's end in the way it used to. Like a drama that cannot be completed in only one hour of TV, when you think you are on the verge of a resolution to the story, a black screen appears with the words, "To be continued…" You are disappointed—you wanted to know the end of the story and were miffed that you'd have to wait and tune in later.

There was a time when my idea of "hell" was each day being like the one before. I need variety and often found it even within the confines of a job. The nature of my work, managing projects, supervising people and writing applications for funds—all of it came with variations. My work always spilled over forcing me to take it home to find uninterrupted time and quiet space for writing. However the hospital in which I worked demanded that all personnel conform with strict beginning and ending times.

That was one reason for resigning from my job and beginning an independent career as a technical writer. Setting my own schedule, working when and how it suited my style and making those days rich with variety. Always in my home office by nine each morning, just to prove I was serious about this business of mine. I loved those days, free and productive.

Some part of today's sameness is imposed upon myself. No matter the time getting to bed my alarm is set for 6:30. Almost two hours before the demands of the day begin with Fritz waking up, this two-hour window of time is set aside just for me. I have a cup of tea, read the morning paper online, read some passages of scripture and often write in my journal. My ritual of walking down the driveway in the first light of a new day, stays the same as when our dog Jake was still alive. The driveway scene is "new every morning," even though it is the same path on the same drive. The light, the temperature, the shadows, the colors are always changing and delighting.

Living in the country with no stores within a twenty-minute drive, a little trip to the grocery store and back would take me an hour. When our kids come for a visit, I don't want to miss out on the diversion they bring to do something practical, like shopping. When they leave it is hard to remain hopeful. Sameness reappears. Great hunks of time are squandered on little, necessary, helpful things. Only I can do this job. My mind restlessly seeks out something different. I have been content to live a quiet life, writing or reading in my upper room. That life is so close but a thousand miles from my day-to-day existence.

One hour of one day every week gives me hope. It is the hour I spend in church. Away from home because of the kindness of four friends, who accepted my request to alternately sit with Fritz while I am gone. He likes to be waiting in his chair when they come and sometimes that makes me late. I slip into a pew trying not to feel conspicuous coming in late, and feeling that all eyes are trained on me. Soon the liturgy and the music hearten me. The bread and wine of communion feed me. Pastor Thea's sermon challenges me. Each word, thought or gesture translates into language directed toward me. Biblical stories are like reading the memoir of a life completely alien to mine. However, they speak to me; I become full of new ideas and rich insight.

Today is one of those ugly winter days. Its steel gray skies could easily overwhelm me. No variation, sameness—like the usual content of my days. When I get home Fritz is so tired from his company he cannot nap peacefully. After helping him to sort things out he is finally quiet. I can also be quiet for a few hours. Time to sort out all these feelings and frustrations; time to count those new blessings even when the days are same-old, same-old.

My heart is full of thanks for the kindness of friends and the blessings of another Sabbath. This is the day and the hour that the Lord has made. What a gift! I will rejoice and be glad in it.

1/13/13

Decision Time

When Amie, our hospice nurse, came for her regular visit she had an answer for Fritz's persistent question: "Is there any way we can speed up this process?" Of course, the process he is talking about is dying.

She suggested we stop most of his medications, over two-dozen a day, all but his anti-rejection meds. Ceasing those drugs would have to be okayed by the hospice doctor and the transplant doctor. A few days later she reported both doctors had approved the medications be discontinued.

Amie explained the option. Without functioning kidneys all the body systems dependent upon their cleaning power would begin to deteriorate—skin, hair, nails, swollen ankles—and those are only the visible ones. Without the anti-rejection meds the disease could accelerate.

The biggest threat to the success of a transplant is rejection of the organ that does not belong to you. Anti-rejection medications must be closely monitored and taken for a person's lifetime. Fritz got blood drawn every other month to determine if the drugs were doing their job, or should be increased or decreased. We did not know that a certain type of cancer can afflict persons like Fritz who depend on drugs to fool the body into thinking the transplanted organ is part of their system.

What we learned quickly once Mantle Cell Lymphoma was diagnosed was that the same drugs which keep his kidney functioning normally came with the cancer risk. Now removing the drugs would be terminal.

Medications had all but stopped—life did not. Fritz had few options for activity. He was too weak to hold his hands up and read a book or newspaper. Television, the old fallback, offered little of interest, even with umpteen channels. His lament and my frustration: there has to be something better than this. No answer. The problem is with the viewer, not the TV.

Times with family over the holidays were rich, if subdued. He did not yearn for more. The life he once knew ended long ago. Fritz was eager for the life after life. While he did not speculate or talk about what heaven may hold, he knows that there will be no more sickness or crying or pain.

So we looked at the possibility of moving more quickly toward that Promised Land. Neither of us took this lightly. Fritz worried that stopping the medication was taking his own life. Amie assured him that the natural processes are at work, and the artificial props that kept his kidneys functioning are now a liability. Useless supports are now standing in the way of the natural course of dying.

Long ago we stated in Living Wills our desire that no artificial means be used to keep us alive in the face of death. Fritz had no need for those listed: a feeding tube, a ventilator, a defibrillator—rescuers, often thought to aid life but often prolonging pain and suffering. Now we see that those extraordinary measures we said we did not want, come in strange disguises.

1/18/13

Last family picture—Thanksgiving, 2012

She made Me Laugh

Today did not begin as a laughing day. It began trying to understand the words of a man, for whom words have become illusive. This is a day I had to prepare him for my leaving, even if only for a few hours: "The hospice aide is coming to give you a bath; sister Mary is coming to help you with lunch and stay while you nap." He resists but I stand my ground. Yes, he says, he understands my need to honor the memory of a friend. Finally I ease out of the house, acting as if there is no rush, but knowing that today's thick fog might slow my trip to town.

The funeral is that of a young woman I knew mostly from her writing. She struggled for many years against cancer. Her blog was filled with life and hope. The funeral is being held in our church, the sanctuary of which will soon be the scene of our own funeral. I could have gotten a recording later and spared myself this shared public grief. I wonder, *why am I putting myself through this?*

Parts of the service make the audience laugh. Her sister and then her father tell stories of her life, with all of her foibles and beauties. She is very real to us now, even those of us who had not been an intimate part of her life. Living with cancer for seven years could not define her—she is so much more. I am jarred by laughter at a funeral.

Then I talk with her mother, a friend from college days, and we cry over the inexplicable loss of a child. I leave with a CD recording of the service and very puffy eyes.

On the way home I make a quick stop to see my daughter, Sue. I need some connection with life after so much thought of death. We share a cup of tea and goodies she made for the kids, and tells me of a book, "A Thousand Gifts," she is using to keep focused on the simple pleasures of life. I smile for maybe the first time that day. Even when she is in turmoil her presence calms me. I love her quest for a peaceful life—I share the search.

The teenagers coming home from school interrupt our peace. My fifteen-year-old granddaughter just experienced the first day of all her classes. She wants to tell all. In her freshman year, she has only one semester under her belt. As she flits about the kitchen searching for food, all the stories came out. Mainly that her teachers are an improvement over the last ones. She can't tame her enthusiasm, especially about her new civics teacher: "Mom, he's a liberal! Now I won't feel so odd."

I laugh at her honesty and am heartened that she finally feels included because of a teacher who may have to mask his own views. She saw his poster of Gandhi. With her artist eye she picked up the visual cues, probably missed by most. She heard him encourage discussion from all sides of topics. I can't help remembering myself feeling alone so long ago in my push for the rights of women. Always looking for persons who dared break tradition. Looking for affirmation of my beliefs, even if from only one. And then finding a way to write what I could not say.

This excited child is the one who repeatedly planted her Obama yard signs in 2008 amid the sea of McCain/Palin signs in her neighborhood—after those signs went mysteriously missing. This is the child who expressed shock at the uniformity of her schoolmates. The child who has watched her parents give their talents for those in need, nearby or in other parts of the world.

So as she eats mom's treats, and then a large bowl of cereal and then a peanut butter bagel after reluctantly putting the Lean Cuisine back into the freezer—I watch and listen. I laugh with delight. Even on the day of a funeral. Even on the day of heaviness as I think about another funeral not too far away. I laugh every time I tell the story.

Driving home I know my husband will be unhappy with me today because I left him—for too long. He will not notice my laughing eyes and the lightness in my voice. He will not see my spirits rise.

Thanks, Tori. Keep that open mind. Keep that infectious spirit. Help your mom create a peaceful home, where people like you are accepted as they are. And yes, keep helping me laugh, even through my tears.

1/30/13

Congrats to Tori—recital

Valentine's Day, 2013

He tells me he loves me. He is tired and somewhat confused but his brow pulls together, tent-like, and his eyes tear. He wants to go to sleep but is suddenly touched by a thought, a feeling, as I sit beside his bed. Words come hard these days: stories without subjects, gaps in sentences and substitutions of fancy words for illusive common ones. But I know what he wants to say before he says it.

Announcing Valentine's Day prompts Fritz to immediately begin talking about Jack, his brother. "Oh, you want Jack to be your valentine?" I tease. He has wanted to talk to his brother but cannot get the confidence to say anything clearly. "Jack already knows you are dying," I say, but it passes over him.

"What would I say?"

"You could just tell him that you love him." For weeks he has been worried about how hard this dying of his will be on his brother. He's trying to protect Jack the way that brothers always do. Surely he loved his brothers long before he loved me.

Like birthdays we have never made much of Valentine's Day. In the past he sometimes gave me a mushy card, but we are not ones to ogle over each other because of a date on the calendar. Maybe that is true of many of those long married. Have we taken our love for granted? Perhaps we don't have to say what both of us know has been the bedrock of our marriage. Maybe just that touch of a hand or an unexpected hug is enough assurance that we are forever joined, "hitched."

In our era of fidelity, at which those younger might be surprised, we never entertained ending our union. We had many a disagreement, some serious, but people of our age and upbringing, rarely considered the default button. Marriage was always a forever kind of thing. So get over the small stuff and carry on. Not that this approach was flawless; some matters dogged us for years. If honest, I will gladly let go of a few of them when death does part us. Today I relearn that a low blouse revealing nothing resembling cleavage, or wearing the casual pants instead of something appropriate for "church," gets his negative attention and comment every single time. Even from his bed he gives me the once-over of acceptability or not, according to his flawless "druthers." I will probably be haunted by that forever.

During the last year and a half I've often thought of the vows we took as green youngsters. "Till death do us part…"

sounded forever away. We were not acquainted with grief, aging, mental decline or sorrow. Each of us was vigorous and ambitious. Together we were serious about life, faith and saw only a bright future. We could not imagine the implications of love during the hard times and especially not when one is dying and the other trying to hang onto a love that is slipping away.

Today I am glad for those non-verbal cues, now that language is fading. The reassuring pat under the covers at night, the touch of a flailing hand finally landing on mine, the pinching of the eyebrows in earnest pain at losing a love. They are better than a card. They are more lasting than flowers. Their sensation lingers on the skin and in images in my mind's eye.

"I love you too—I always have," I say. And his eyes smile just a little. That look washes away all the pain of the last year, all the fatigue of today and all our unresolved differences. Being "one" was never easy. But saying before God and the people who care about us that we "do" make that pledge, however naïve, leads us to this Valentine's Day. It even brings us to a moment of parting with a sense of joy. All these years rolled into one quiet expression, "I love you—and I always will."

2/14/13

Last Haircut

"Ok Fritz, you owe me $3,330 for haircuts that you have charged to my account."

And that is at the modest rate of ten dollars per cut because I am not a professional. I did cut hair while in college,

Chris with Grandpa

when the styles turned short and women needed trims more often. The cuts were cheap and convenient and may have been passable, although I remember doing a poor job once and seeing the woman and her botched haircut repeatedly around campus. I prayed for fast growth.

In school-picture after school-picture I see the uneven bangs on the heads of our children. As soon as they exerted a choice, they did not come to this hairdresser. I was one of the few moms that welcomed longer hair in boys because my son was hard to please.

You were not hard to please, Fritz—you opted for convenience.

I don't remember him as fussy at first. He needed that last minute haircut for some occasion and knew he could count on me to give in and grudgingly say "OK" to a late night demand. His reasoning: *Why make an appointment when you live with the woman who cuts your hair? Hey, the scissors are there so what is holding us back? And she knows the way you like it done.*

He got exactly three cuts from someone else in our fifty-three years together. The one I love to tease him about is the one he got in Japan, while there on a professional trip. Some of his friends probably talked him into it. Only later did I realize that the cut came with lots more services!

I have had many years to perfect the Fritz cut. Since the buzz cut he had when we met, and after the long hair era of the 70s, he has settled on a standard cut. Over the years his hair changed color and texture. At first it was slightly wavy and thick. It thinned and lightened until it became a distinguished gray but the styling was always the same, give or take a few years of long sideburns. I was pleased that I could keep Fritz trimmed and looking good.

Twice the texture of his hair changed from soft and manageable to straight and lifeless. During the time in which he learned that his kidneys were failing, his hair and many other parts of his outward appearance changed. All those toxins in the blood stream even compromised his hair and scalp. And now as he is slowly dying of cancer of the lymph system, his hair has changed again. His silver gray is now steelier. The hair is coarse and lifeless once again.

In the past few years he has taken to being very directive while I am cutting his hair. He points out parts that really need attention. He warns me that because his hair is thinning, I must take care not to remove too much in the places he

"You may take my picture" – New Year's Eve, 2012

needs cover—the receding hairline and his front wave I call a du-op. He does not remember that I know the landscape of his head of hair better than I know my own. His preferences are burned into my psyche.

A month ago he sat on the kitchen stool while I cut his hair. It was hard because keeping his body upright and his head erect took so much energy. After the hurry–up cut, he flopped back in bed. I wondered if that would be the last haircut, as he seemed to be failing so fast. But Fritz has defied all expectations of his decline and yesterday it was time for another haircut.

He no longer washes his own hair but he would never let another, even me, comb it. Hc has this method of combing it down, Donald Trump like, parting it and pushing each side back with his brush. Then he carefully lays a comb on top and gently pushes the top forward and down until he has created his classic du-op. Of course the front wave, which now nicely covers a bare forehead, would never stay unless sprayed with "Veffus," a name his kids gave his hairspray long ago. He uses only one kind and panics if he cannot find the product. He cuts the spray with water so that the wave looks natural, not plastered. But, he can go out in any weather, and when others hair is mussed up, his still stays in place. It almost feels like a hairpiece.

You would think that a guy who is mostly in bed would not think haircut. But his occasional ride into the bathroom facing the large mirror, make him think otherwise. He hates seeing the "pillow hair" sticking up like Woody Woodpecker in the back. "Cut it off," he orders but I insist that it would make the rest of his head look strange. As the locks became ever more upright he wanted a haircut. Several days we tried to make it happen but he begged off because of tiredness. Yesterday I kind of gave him an ultimatum—now or never. He wanted to defer because of tiredness but I said he only had to sit and I would do all the work.

At first he was sure I needed his directions. But soon even that got too wearying. So I cut like I was in a race. I gave him a kind of brush cut in the back but carefully preserved the frontal view. Quickly trimming above the ears and smoothing the neck with the razor before his endurance timer went off and he needed to get back in bed. Oh, my, but he could not leave without sculpting the du-op and applying the Veffus. His last best effort brought back the look he worked so hard to maintain his whole lifelong.

His steel gray hair was everywhere, some outside of the neck towel. But he never complained of itch nor commented about something not being quite right. Maybe I am finally going to be trusted to do the job he wants. Normal has been restored.

I am glad we had long ago chosen cremation instead of embalming. No one could ever get that du-op just right.

2/18/13

Fritz's 60 birthday

CHAPTER THREE

MIDNIGHT

Reflection

The holidays we never expected to share, Thanksgiving, Christmas, New Year's Day, and Valentine's Day, came and went, with unexpected moments of joy in each. On New Year's Eve Fritz surprised me by saying that I could take his picture. Perhaps this was his way to say goodbye while he still looked okay. Wearing his gray MSU sweatshirt and sitting in his black chair, he smiled just a little at my urging.

Most of our family can come and go at will and drop by the house when they have free time. They know we are stationary here in the country. They know if they don't bring food, I will always rustle up a meal. Son Doug lives the farthest away and also needs a driver to get here. Between work, school, sports and finding time on a weekend that his kids are with him, his visits are harder to come by. In mid-February it worked for him to come with his three children on a Saturday. So often when they come, the house is full of cousins, aunts and uncles—lots of activity. But on this day, the only agenda was to spend time with Grandpa Fritz.

Fritz was in great form that day. I tilted the bed so he could sit up facing Doug, Brian, Marielle and Morgan. He looked

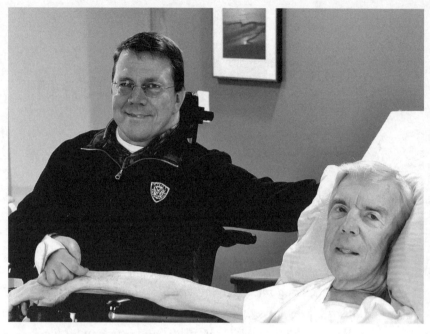

Father and son

almost healthy as he laughed and talked with the kids. His hair was perfect!

Lunch was served in the bedroom so we could all eat together. It was not a feast but festive nonetheless. No one was in a hurry to leave. Two hours into the visit, Fritz admitted he was tired and would have to take a nap. Hugs and kisses were exchanged before the Rottman family took their leave, carrying sweet memories with them.

A few days later, Pastor Thea and an elder from church came to serve us Holy Communion. We gathered around his bed, using the over-bed tray as our communion table, set with bread and wine. A candle flickered as we shared the body and blood of Christ. Grace filled our hearts and the whole room glowed. Looking back, that event seems like his "last rites."

Still Waiting

Winter may be the hardest part of waiting. Losing ones bearings, is like being lost in a snow-covered woods without a compass and surrounded by identical looking trees. After the holidays were over, we entered the January and then February darkness. The absence of change left us hard pressed to see we had advanced toward the inevitable end. It was a lonely limbo for both of us—so tired of body and mind.

The waiting had a deadening effect. Fritz's life was now reduced to a bed. For the past three days he has gotten up only to take two steps to the portable commode chair and back. The trips by wheelchair to the bathroom proved too cumbersome, with four transfers to accomplish the job at hand. Weak muscles make for unsteady ups and downs.

He has a medicine pump, the line of which is attached to his leg and has to be protected from pulls. Once he got up in the middle of night, and tried to get to the bathroom unaided, he strained the line. This required an on-call hospice nurse to move the lead to his belly so it was more manageable though still irritating to him. Later it got its third location on the other leg. If he turned in the night and restricted the cord, an alarm like the paparazzi went off and I was forced to get up and find the cause.

The medicine pump was installed to solve another problem. He was anxious all the time about forgetting the magic formula for feeling good. When frustrated he often directed anger at me. Arguing with a big man who is not thinking clearly in the middle of the night is scary. I have given into some wild things to avoid confrontation. One night we walked around the living room at 2 a.m. because he was certain it would help him void. He draped himself around my shoulder as we moved from bed to chair and back to bed, carrying his medicine pump in a plastic bag.

The doctor predicted his appetite would diminish once the medicine was continuous. Not so. Waking in the morning he looks for his standard breakfast of a bowl of oatmeal followed by a bowl of cold cereal. An hour later he may complain that he hasn't had anything to eat. Other meals are small but usually eaten completely. One good thing is I can serve him the same meal each lunch and supper and it will seem new to him.

I have lost my own interest in eating and many other things. I rarely sit down to write, because the open time is short. I no longer go outside each morning as soon as the sun comes up. Predicting his needs became unpredictable. Making to-do lists too frustrating. Just keeping the finances straight and the family informed about all that is happening is about all I can do. Yet I often feel like I am busy doing nothing.

Long ago I planned the funeral when the prognosis was weeks to months. Later when they withdrew all his standard meds, the estimate was revised again: days to weeks. I wrote his obituary and made a decision about a funeral home. Nothing is finalized.

Fritz no longer rests in the promises he has always held dear. I pray for that peace in dying he professed when first getting the diagnosis. I pray for his home-going now that he cannot imagine any life but the one he struggles through right now. Together we pray: God take him—soon.

When he dies it will not be the beginning of my grief. For years I have cried over the loss of his beautiful mind. The signs came slowly but relentlessly. Each piece that fell shattered like broken glass. How could such a creative man be reduced to shards? Now he is asking, "what time is it?" every few minutes. He is surprised when I say the name of the nurse that has helped him for over four months—"who?" The name Amie, the one who comes every week, does not ring a bell. Several things remain—thankfulness and appreciation. His default "thanks" mode makes helpers think that he is really on top of things.

I may be depressed. People come or call and they brighten an hour. When the person walks out the door, I think, "now what?" I have never felt so alone—so trapped. I am losing my creative mind if not my mind altogether. Nothing seems important. Nothing bright. The beautiful words in a book, the hymns that are always playing in my mind, the messages from sermons quickly wash away. I look at the book I wrote on the coffee table, *All Nature Sings,* and cannot hear any music. Comfort flees. Gloom sets in, especially toward the end of the day. How will I make it through another evening with a man who has completely lost interest in the world he inhabits?

2/22/13

Another Kind of Waiting

Hours after my last writing, everything changed. Fritz ate two meals, breakfast and lunch, in quick succession and welcomed visits from both nurse Amie and aide Cassie. Amie started a new port for medicine because the old one was inflamed and Cassie washed his hair. He looked brand new. Then he went to sleep.

When he didn't wake in a few hours, I tried to rouse him by opening the shades and doing chores around him. I speculated that he was exhausted from all the attention but

Hiking among the discarded blocks of Marble (Marble quarry)

was wrong. He was beginning a deep sleep. We were now in new territory. He seemed too tired to eat. Too tired to drink. No interest in the TV news. He just wanted to sleep. By nine he was asleep for the night. I joined him.

He woke several times with the urge to pee. Once I helped him to the commode but with little success. He seemed unsteady, and he just flopped back down on the bed. Several times his legs slid off the bed and I had to go round and put them back up. By morning he was halfway down on the bed with his feet hanging off. I got a chair to make a bed extension.

I wondered how to get Fritz's lead weight back up in bed when I heard neighbor Bruce shoveling snow off our walk.

I popped my head out the door and asked if he'd be willing to help move Fritz into position. Together we used the draw sheet. Fritz woke briefly to thank Bruce and was back to sleep.

Later he insisted again he get up to use the commode. I tried to dissuade him because I feared Bruce's move would soon be wasted. He became agitated in a way that always scares me—so I complied. He hardly made the turn and sat before peeing on the rug beside the bed, unable to sit far enough back on the chair. I struggled to get him back in bed when I discovered that he had already soiled the sheets. I had to pull the wet stuff from under him and try to replace the soiled underwear with a disposable pair. While trying to solve this problem, both his legs slid off the bed again. I helped him sit up, but it didn't work—he was again crosswise. I stepped into the bathroom for more pads when he got up again and promptly crumpled to the floor.

I laid him out with a pillow under his head and covered him with a blanket. He seemed content to lie there. I called hospice for help. They suggested I call a neighbor but by now Bruce was at work. Hospice does not permit personnel to lift patients so they suggested I call 911 non-emergency. While waiting for someone to respond, I changed the bed. Two nice young people came and had Fritz back in bed in no time. He roused again and thanked them profusely. How long would this "in bed" last?

I asked the hospice weekend nurse to bring a Foley catheter so Fritz would not have to get out of bed again. I took their suggestion and requested a hospital bed. I had been dreading another night of uncertainty so was relieved knowing the bed rails would be up and Fritz would not fall on the floor.

Daughter Barb was set to spend the night so we could transfer Fritz to the new arrangement; also something hospice is not allowed to do. Her husband came home early from out of town to help. Together they lifted him from the wheelchair to the bed, which we set up in the dining room. Finally Fritz was in this safe bed-home.

With Fritz confined between the side rails, he could neither hurt himself nor me. He never reacted one way or another to his new place. Except for one feisty night, so sure he had to get someplace "right now," he has settled in for the duration.

Now, it is clear he will die in this bed. So after fifty-three years of sharing the same bed with this man almost every night, the new sleeping arrangement is a prelude to the ways my life will change. Will I still wake up every few hours wondering if he needs me? Who will need me when he is gone?

Everything in me says, "no," "stop," "not yet!" I don't want him to go; I want him to go. The long wait suddenly seems too short. The pain of losing him makes my chest tighten and my mind spin. Death is so final.

Our youngest daughter came to stay with me. Sue's gentle spirit soothed my troubled heart. It has now been four days since his body decided it had had enough. I never imagined this kind of end to the story of our life together. He sleeps continually. Last night I could rouse his interest for a while by naming all our children and grandchildren and saying something about each. Tonight I spent an hour trying to

Carol with fiancée in Denver 1958

get his attention by singing hymns but no response. If he hears me, I cannot tell, as there is no change of expression or opening of eyes.

Although his mind decided long ago it was time to go, in his body the fight continued. Suddenly they are together in longing to "be done with the troubles of this world." Now I know it will be soon. No one can live without eating or drinking. He desires neither. Our prayers have been answered. Jesus is coming quickly. Rest in peace, my dear Fritz.

2/25/13

Resting after a long hike

The Bed

I have no story
to tell
of the final days
in our communal bed.

Hazy memories of marriage beginnings,
no marked mid-point—
now the unceremonious end.

Alone, I recall the cozy space
the hushed tones
the back rubs
the moon glow
and then sweet sleep.

The shared life
of souls entwined
through hell and high water
striving toward paradise at low tide.

Side by side
Now touching,
now going separate ways
'til at day's end,
always meeting
in the bed.

C. Rottman,

9/7/13

TOMORROW

Jeeping in Marble

A NEW DAWN

Reflection

With the memorial service looming, my children honored my wishes to be alone. They kept in constant touch, in case I changed my mind. Most tasks could wait but one thing could not: my mind and my heart needed to process the happenings of the past year. No other person required my attention—except me. I'm thankful for a time to mourn.

My mind filled with those final moments: our family gathering around his deathbed; the hospice nurse confirming what we already knew; the black coats carrying his body to the hearse; prayers uttered by emotionally exhausted people who loved Fritz dearly. Some moments are too personal to be written and will be treasured only in memory.

His was a "good death." With the help of caring doctors who were not afraid to talk about death, hospice workers who were comfortable with dying, and people in our community of faith who upheld us with wishes and prayers—Fritz was able to die at home, free of medical intervention, cared for by those who he loved. Years ago when we wrote our living will, this is just what we hoped for: a peaceful parting.

During those days, I entertained some of the same questions I ponder today while completing this chapter of our life with memoir. What was the essence of his life? How can I honor this good man? Will I survive without him? There may be no answers—only questions. I think about our coming together, the act of becoming "we" not two "I's." Relationships seem to be at the heart of this book. When you commit your life to another you know only what is apparent at the time. None of us know what we will do when we "alteration find," either the prospect of death or the dying of a relationship.

When I finally dared to look back at what I had written over three years of intense change in our togetherness, I was surprised. Anger, sadness, pain at being misunderstood, longing for an end, moments of doubt that God was even present. I see no heroism, no guidance—nothing but reality. That may be all I have to offer: just words about our long road together; just words that show that love never fails even through a thousand little deaths and the final parting.

The epilogue that follows is a review of the end of our life together; forgive me for repeating some facts, as I try to make sense of his final days and our shared journey. Know that each day I am convinced by these words from the hymn, Amazing Grace:

"'Tis Grace that brought me safe thus far,
and Grace will lead me home."

Can You See the Prairie?

I am seated at the dining room table in the room where Fritz died. The place that was my downstairs workspace for most of the days of his illness. It is a Danish modern table we bought in Sweden decades ago and still sits in the middle under a hanging light. For one week this room housed a hospital bed, a chair on either side and an over-the-bed table.

When CareLink brought the bed, I asked the delivery crew to position it with the foot end next to the window, still hoping Fritz would enjoy an outside view as well as the hanging leaded-glass art in front of the window. Looking back, it was too late to concern myself with how he was positioned. He was safe in his walled bed with no imperative to get to the bathroom. That was when I understood we were both adapting and peacefully accepting his last dwelling place on earth. Together, we had reached the beginning of the end.

Sitting in this room brings back Fritz's last words. After all the moving to and resettling into the new bed, he welcomed daughter Barb's presence into the evening at his bedside. From deep in his memory, he recited the entire Lord's Prayer with her. The busyness of the day caught up to me. On my way to bed I stopped to say goodnight. He turned his head slightly toward me and said clearly, "I love you." He met my eyes and spoke those precious words. It was our final goodbye.

On his last day our granddaughter Dani came to see him. Her parents were not sure she could handle it, because now his mouth was open most of the time and his eyes closed. With twelve-year-old determination, she insisted. With her dad she sat beside Grandpa's bed and held his hand. She greeted him in her sweet clear voice. He opened his eyes momentarily and she felt a connection. In the tiniest of ways, he reached back to her.

The artwork hangs on the window, catching sunlight through colorful pieces of glass. The prairie beyond is just waking up from its winter sleep. Nothing ever really dies.

Wildflower

In Memorium: Fritz M. Rottman, March 29,1937 — March 2, 2013

The Silhouette Season

Bright colors of dancing flame fade to embers

when leaves announce the finale
of the growing, mellow-warm, life-giving season
and let go, spinning and drifting down.

Layers of gorgeous debris delight us
with crackle and crunch in a patchwork
of startling color—a crazy, changing quilt,
we want to hold from turning a monotone brown.

Saved leaves delight, then curl, all spotted brittle
in the trash. Last holdouts of oak and willow
finally join the forest's carpet, blending
gold and crimson in a hearty winter soup.

At first light or day's last glow the naked trees stand
unashamed in the distance, without costume or
curtain. Not even a fig leaf hides their skinny
shaking limbs, reaching desperately heavenward.

Crayon art rounds branches with mandatory leaves,
supplying what no longer hangs, as if a
tree is not a tree without its clothes. But life buds
inside, growing a ringed mark in winter's dark chill.

The silhouette season—melancholy, brooding, lonely—
a colorless contrast, of beautifully bleak timber,
in the vast shadowbox of life: completely awake,
stoking the fire-glow within.

C. Rottman (from <u>All Nature Sings</u>)

Autumn Glow – Life's Theme for Fritz

Each morning I read a poem on The Writer's Almanac. One called *Autumn* caught my eye, drawing me in with a quote from John Donne, "In heaven is it always Autumn." That became the theme of the memorial service for Fritz. For me, he will live forever in autumn glow.

The autumn of 2012 may have been the loveliest ever experienced—or at least it seemed so. We carried the weight of gloom within our hearts while outside the landscape glowed with color. The dread of bad news confronted by intense beauty. A hymn played in my mind: "How can my heart be sad?...God reigns, let the earth be glad!"

The day we drove to Greenville to confer with the hematologist was an exceptionally glorious. All the autumn's brilliance rode with us. The sunlight tilted off the hanging leaves, gave no hint of trouble.

Soon we had a name for the trouble and its prognosis of "weeks to months." With the days remaining, Fritz wanted more of the fall; he wanted to take a "color tour."

It would have been fitting for Fritz to go down in the autumn blaze of glory, but he lingered through the winter. Winter did not define him even as death overtook him. His season was autumn when all the work of summer was finally over. His crops gathered, the garden prepared to over-winter

Granddaughter Lindsay and grandpa at Bay Cliff Health Camp for children in UP

and tools neatly organized in the barn—he could rest from his labors. Usual but unexpected joy lingered in nature. Many a cool day in the past autumns, he photographed the beauties of goldenrod and aster, monarchs on prairie coneflowers and the crimson dogwood leaves. He recorded the fruits of his garden labor: winter squash drying in the sun, late season raspberries, bunches of crisp carrots.

On one of his last trips outside, bundled in a down jacket and sitting on the porch swing, he delighted in watching the last of the dry oak leaves flying horizontally in front of us. The sun set over the distant woods through cloud-dotted skies. Cold weather ended the autumn glow.

Autumn was never the end; Fritz's farmer's heart always watched for signs of cyclical change. In January he poured over seed catalogues planning for next year's planting and harvest. Vivaldi's *Four Seasons* was always his first choice while sitting in his easy chair. The orchestral sounds reminded him that one season always follows another. And in the words of the fiddler, "Filled with happiness and tears."

The funeral bulletin used the words of John Donne, Fritz's picture of a bed of autumn leaves and another of his beloved butterfly weed superimposed with these familiar words:

"Great is thy faithfulness…
Summer and winter, springtime and harvest,
Sun, moon and stars in their courses above,
Join with all nature in manifold witness
To Thy great faithfulness, mercy and love…
All I have needed thy hand hath provided.
Great is Thy faithfulness, Lord, unto me!

A friend wrote this poem, which may best define Fritz's life.

A Writer's Prayer in Autumn

Creator God,
Thank you for that tree,
the small one, with low

branches holding tight
to its leaves, orange
fringed with yellow,
fiery tongues suspended
from brittle stems.

And around that tree,
the small one, circled thick
trunks with bare limbs,
a company of quiet maples,
empty and still
after layering
the grass gold.

Forgive me for only slowing
my hurried pace,
forgive me
I should have stopped,
taken off my shoes
and knelt.
But I rushed on
to important things,
things I have now forgotten.

Give me the eyes
to notice and let
my words catch
color and flame,
fall and float
brightly on a page,
so I may stand
empty handed,
pointing to you.

Otto Selles

The Stash

Fritz liked to think of himself as frugal; he enjoyed the comment that his lifestyle never changed although it could have. He would point to his closet and remark that he spent little on clothes since moving to Michigan in 1999. He forgot about those times when he couldn't find a certain type of shirt and would say, "I'm going to get a bunch of those," and hurried away with the mail order catalogue. He worried I would not be frugal when he was gone. Each time I wore something he thought was new he'd worry about my spending habits. Some were items I had not worn in years and others were purchased long ago with the sale tag still attached.

At the memorial service for Fritz, when son Doug spoke the collected memories of the siblings, he recalled that when they were growing up, each proposed purchase was met with the words, "Do you think that would be stewardly?" He was especially skeptical of those "must haves" with the labels that made a certain shoe or pair of jeans precious to a preteen. Fritz, like many of our generation, looked aghast at prices of goods that once were half that price and, of course, twice as good.

As the children, grandchildren and I looked through all of his belongings in order to find them other homes, we had many a laugh over the things he could never get enough of: batteries of all sizes, flashlights, sun hats, baseball caps, fishing vests, jackets of all types, some dating back to our early years together. Oh, and there were the dozens of pocketknives, pens, paperclips, note cards and sticky notes. One of the kids remarked, "If you need something don't go to Costco, come to Fritz's warehouse first!" He had built shelves in our storeroom to house all the "big lots" of paper towels, toilet paper and soft soap refill liquid. Since he did not visit the storeroom before shopping, he would insist that we were almost out of an item, only to double up. He didn't know that I secretly brought supplies to our children to relieve the overflow.

There were also the big-ticket items. Cars—he never skimped on type and amenities once he decided on the best value from Consumer's Report. Then he conveniently forgot the purchase price, always underestimating it in his memory. He might skimp on some things, but when he needed a new tractor to work on the land he went all-out on a new John Deere. Once the deal was made, without consultation I might add, he conveniently forgot just what it cost. There was no price too high for a good machine. He used it infrequently but enjoyed every minute of brush hogging the fields, his skin protected from sunlight by the little canopy. The farmer in him sweated and beamed.

His two favorite stores were Costco and Lowe's. He loved to think he was saving money, even when he came home with hundreds of dollars of things he was sure were a good deal, even though he had never compared the prices anywhere else. He loved to go through the little Costco sale brochure they sent by mail and circle the coupons for things that we could certainly use. I hated to say, "we have enough of that or we never use that," because it ruined his saving-spree.

He made trip after trip to Lowe's because he thought he needed a certain item—and came home with so much more. He always looked for one salesman who was particularly good at selling him sprays and pellets to fight his enemies, the chipmunks and the rabbits.

Fasteners, screws, nails, light bulbs, and gloves. He loved gloves; could hardly throw the old ones away even as the new ones piled up. There was only one thing he lacked, later in life—organization. He had so many tools that at one time he thought he should put a color-code on three sets, one for house, one for garage and one for barn. I am sure Fritz's dad warned his son, as Fritz later did to his, to "put things back where you found them." In his haste Fritz never did that. He thought it would be helpful if each had a distinctive color painted or taped to it, so he'd know where it belonged.

One summer he hired granddaughter Lindsay to help him organize. She did a bang up job. In the basement workroom they hung pegboard and attached umpteen items to hooks where they could be seen more easily. She could not convince him to get rid of the duplicates. She sorted the screws by like kinds and gathered the screwdrivers, wrenches and types of tape together. In his study she figured out his groupings and labeled the file drawers by their contents. They made many more labels, creating new files so everything would have a place. Even I could find things now, but Fritz complained each time he misplaced something—sure that Lindsay had put it in a strange place. The summer before they had done the same thing in the barn. They also put a cabinet together to store things by type in the garage. The arrangement did not last. It was redone and just recently, redone again. Too much stuff: more gloves, multiple types of fertilizers and repellents, nozzles, hand tools, cords. We may not have to return to Lowe's for years.

But all of his stuff did not represent work. Fritz had a weakness for fireworks; he loved to buy them even though he had a fear of lighting them. The kids remember so many safety warnings on the 4th of July on the beach that some of

Grandchildren backpacking.

the fun was gone. Later he used the small "bottle rockets" to frighten the geese off our dock. He'd put the stick end in a Coke bottle, light it and aim it from the deck. The rocket flew in a big arch and banged right over their heads. Mad scurrying into the water—smiles from the deck. He lamented that he had no such scare tactic for the chipmunks.

Soon after Fritz died, I found a large, dusty bag of fireworks on the top shelf in the clothes closet. And then one in the laundry room, the storeroom and the workroom—all stowed in brown paper bags out of sight. The grandkids collected them in one big pile, amazed that their cautious Grandpa Fritz would have dangerous things like this in his house. I turned them over to the kids when they told me they thought that Uncle Doug should have them.

On the night after Fritz's funeral we gathered at daughter Barb's house to decompress and remember. All of a sudden, there were loud bangs and flashes outside the window. The shadowy forms of the teenagers moved back and forth in the dusk. They lit all the fireworks as one extravagant tribute to Grandpa Fritz. I like to think of it as our version of an Irish Wake.

A month later, we found another stash, while emptying his hunting closet. Someone spirited the brown bag away. Next year they will probably shoot another tribute skyward, in memory of the frugal guy who thought he watched his pennies while loving and hoarding many priceless treasures.

5/21/13

Marble Revisited

"Gonna' take a sentimental journey..."

That's the tune that ran through my head as I boarded the plane, heading for Aspen and eventually Marble, Colorado. Fritz and I had come to the Crystal River Valley together ever since our honeymoon in the summer of 1959. Even though we never lived in Colorado as a family, all of our children, their spouses and finally all our grandchildren have come to this place from birth onward. There are more vacation homes dotting the mountainsides now but the town remains a sleepy little town frequented by trout fishermen, mountain bikers, backpackers and a few permanent residents. The main distinction of Marble is that it happens to be one of the most beautiful places on earth.

On the other side of the Treasury Mountain Range one will find Aspen: bustling, busy, glitzy. Only a good hour's drive separates Aspen from Marble but the two are light-years away. In Aspen you might sight a famous person or go to the legendary Woody Creek Tavern or hear a famous musician or group. We prefer "down home" Marble, where you can just be yourself and make your own fun.

Fritz loved to fish and anticipated being on the Crystal River or at Beaver Lake for months before a trip. His heart beat a little faster when we started down the last five-mile stretch of dirt road to the cabin.

Our first child was an infant when we took our first backpacking excursion. That was before the sport became popular and the consumer-friendly, lightweight equipment available. Our gear came from an Army/Navy surplus store in Baltimore. Fritz also carried a paperback copy of *The Rise and Fall of the Third Reich,* and a handgun in case of a bear attack. As novice hikers tramping uphill, we carried far more weight on our backs than any sane person should.

Our years were planned around the annual trip to Marble. Backpacking now included the whole family, sharing the load. During those years, eight grandchildren were introduced to this beautiful part of the country. Each of them loved the place as we did and found their own adventures, more exciting than we ever imagined.

As the summer of 2012 came, we all knew our travel plans would have to accommodate Fritz's weakening body. Within the span of a year, he had the strange swelling of his tongue, major surgery, radiation and was not regaining strength as we hoped. To match his activities to his energy level, teenagers Matt and Chris drove him to fish and tour the area so he could see all the old familiar places. He sat on the porch of the cabin watching the kids whittle sticks or carve marble chunks, and told them old stories. One night

Daughter Barb hiking with her dad

we looked through old photographs and videos from the past summers. Some of the videos were made in Marble the year before, showing the exploits of the grandchildren. Fritz expressed concern for their "risk taking" while telling stories of his own risky behavior when he was that age. He was impressed by their film record of all their fun and lamented that his own wild adventures were never recorded.

Despite travel woes, it was a great year in Marble for all of us—most importantly for Fritz. We had no idea it would be his last.

In October Fritz got the diagnosis of incurable cancer. We wanted badly to help grant his last wish to return to

Marble—once more. But his bodily weakness soon curtailed any travel, even close to home. The kids came to see him often rehearsing all the old Marble legends.

Fritz died in March. Perhaps his vision of heaven looked very much like Marble. It was the place he felt closest to God. I remember his delight as he walked through the pines and among the wild flowers, watched the moon shows ending in alpenglow and the sky sometimes full of periodic, momentary shooting stars. Maybe he can still feel the native rainbow trout tugging at his line in the Crystal River.

Each family member has and will continue to grieve in his/her own way. They, too, have made memories with him in Marble. I will continue to share tears with everyone who loved him, but for now I wanted a space to be sentimental and simply cry—alone.

I took this maiden voyage to Marble in the late spring, so I would have unhurried time to bring back all the images of our years here together. He is everywhere in the place. I traced his path up the hill and down. He planted his last steps here less than a year ago, pushing himself to set one foot in front of the other. It must have been like carrying a double heavy backpack, but he was determined he would make it to the top of the mountain—as always.

5/20/13

Shall we gather at the river?

I've asked the whole family to meet me on the bank of the Crystal River—the river that runs through Marble forming the valley between mountains of the Treasury Mountain range. As a mountain stream it is close to its tributaries and swells and rolls in spring; by midsummer it calms to a placid

Kids start backpacking young with a dog's help.

waterway. From time to time, storms in the high country muddy the usually crystal-clear waters.

Our meeting place is "the beach," a flat gravely space where the Carbonate Creek tumbles down into the Crystal. The kids spend hours playing on the beach between swims. I pick the spot because we can drive the old Jeep onto the beach, which allows Doug to ride, where his wheelchair cannot go.

This gathering is a near miracle: my three children, spouses and all eight grandchildren along with several cousins and a friend are present at one time in one place for one purpose. We meet here to spread ashes—of our grandpa, dad, uncle and husband in one of his favorite places, a trout stream in the Crystal River Valley where Fritz loved to fish. There is no more fitting place of rest for his ashes.

We form a circle next to the jeep, while I read these words from Psalm 121:

> I lift up my eyes to the hills—
> from where will my help come?
>
> My help comes from the Lord,
> who made heaven and earth.
>
> He will not let your foot be moved;
> he who keeps you will not slumber.
>
> He who keeps Israel
> will neither slumber nor sleep.
>
> The Lord is your keeper;
> the Lord is your shade at your right hand.
>
> The sun shall not strike you by day,
> nor the moon by night.
> The Lord will keep you from all evil;
> he will keep your life.
>
> The Lord will keep
> your going out and your coming in
> from this time on and for evermore.

(NRSV)

The passage remains a favorite in this mountainous place, but even as I speak the words, its talk of protection seems strange as we gather to memorialize the loss of a man to death. "The Lord will keep you from all evil; he will keep your life." The truth is, all of us continue to trust the one who holds the world in his hands. We will not defy death or accident but we will forever feel secure.

Many in the circle tell the stories that endear Fritz to them. He taught some to fish, some to laugh at his quirky rendering of familiar rhymes, some to respect all people no matter their station in life, some to garden, some to be generous with everything they have. The love stories reveal a man with a large presence in their lives. The memories we share celebrate his life; this common ground will forever be hallowed.

One of the group reads a quote from Norman McLean's famous book, *A River Runs Through It*.

"…all things merge into one, and a river runs through it.
The river was cut by the world's great flood and runs
over rocks from the basement of time.
On some of the rocks are timeless raindrops.
Under the rocks are the words, and some of the words are
theirs.
I am haunted by waters."

Now, one by one starting with the youngest, each takes a scoop of ashes to the river's edge and pours it in. There is a little shoal into the river and Doug is driven into the water so he too can toss the ashes of his father. I love them all more than ever as they honor Fritz. As the oldest I take my scoop of ashes to the place where the water runs over the rocks as

The eight grandchildren gathering at the Crystal River to spread Grandpa's ashes.

the Carbonate Creek and the Crystal River join, mingling their waters.

We join hands and sing, "Praise God from whom all blessings flow. Praise him all creatures here below. Praise him above all heavenly hosts. Praise Father, Son and Holy Ghost. Amen."

"Shall we gather at the river? Where bright angel's feet have trod.

With its Crystal tide forever flowing by the throne of God.

Yes! We'll gather at the river—the beautiful the beautiful river.

Gather with the saints at the river, that flows by the throne of God."

The Puzzle

LIFE AFTER PARTING: LITTLE RAYS OF HOPE

Reflection

When my father died over thirty years ago, my siblings and I inherited about one hundred pages of Memoir, carefully typed by my mother. I also saved ten years of his day-books, in which he recorded the minutia of his days. I vowed to begin the practice. I soon found writing only one page a day, too restrictive but writing every day, guilt producing. Now I use large lined books that open flat, and write when I need to. The need has been great since Fritz died. I roamed through the Psalms looking for courage to go on.

This morning I found the following entry written exactly a year ago:

Those who sow in tears
will reap with songs of joy
He who goes out weeping,
carrying seeds to sow,
will return with songs of joy,
carrying sheaves with him.

Psalm 126:5-6

"This whole 'finding a new life' is a process—slow, deliberate—work while you weep—and finally joy will come. Not all at once but ever so slowly. I think of when Fritz and I first scatter-seeded the prairie along the driveway—just like old-fashion sowers with a small pouch over the shoulder with an opening at hand level. Grab a handful of wildflower seeds and throw them out to fall on the land. The process took only part of a day but the results we hoped for took years.

I sowed the seeds with expectation not tears, but many a time I wanted to cry from the longing for the flowers that were reluctant to bloom. Some part of me stopped believing that the seeds would ever germinate.

Five years later, I could pick a sheaf of wild flowers when walking down the long drive. Coreopsis, prairie cone flowers, and purple vervain greeted me. I chose to leave them in the wild but carried the joy of their being with me.

Today I am sowing with tears. I don't even know what seeds are germinating right now. I wait in expectation, with faith that in due time I will once again reap a harvest I can sing about."

12/11/13

Life is Fragile

I'm at Fran's house sharing a few minutes together on a rainy Thursday in East Lansing. We have been longing to see each other since Fritz died. So after driving son Doug to a conference we had our moments. She has been in the same place I am now even though it has been several years since Chuck died. Some of the things that draw us together are the same as they have always been: crusading for women's rights; caring about people, she as an empathetic social worker and

I as a teacher. She was always one of the most hopeful people I knew, good humored and wise.

She and Chuck were instinctively gracious to us—inviting Doug to spend nights when he came back to East Lansing to see his high school buddies after his accident. Sometimes there were late nights. Chuck was always there to put out his board ramps in the garage and help lift Doug into bed.

Fran and I are different in many ways, but after talking to her for an hour, I see that she, like me, is also a very practical sort of woman. We know how to "just deal with it" when troubles come.

Before Chuck was diagnosed with ALS, I never saw that side of her. She was a proper sort of person; always dressing well and raising her children to be polite and welcoming to guests. Some of this I attributed to her upbringing in a household of Dutch immigrants. There is an Old World flavor to her graciousness.

Fritz and I visited them several times after hearing of Chuck's diagnosis. During years of a hoarse voice and then a cough that would not got away, they knew that something was going wrong. I don't know if this was their first real brush with crisis, but they met it with extraordinary determination. Fran and her adult children would do what they could to make the rest of Chuck's days as good as could be. They had their parties, Chuck went to work with help, and they amassed the technology so he could communicate as long as possible. We witnessed his artificial voice saying what his mind knew we would be interested in. Fran got attendant help so she could maintain some semblance of the life she knew as a therapist.

Back when our son was injured over thirty years ago and we did not know if he would live, Fran was the first person by my side. She insisted that we go out for lunch at a nice place. She showed me a model of normalcy she knew would be hard to find then and in the years to come. I missed her when we left East Lansing for Cleveland and we seldom saw each other. Now I am in trouble and I seek her out again.

This time I am the one who has to live without my husband. I must learn how to live again. There are other widows I know but none like Fran and none with such a long shared history. She knows about the long slow decline of a husband and all the things a wife must do just to survive until his end: finances and management and communication and everything in between. One gains strength by doing those hard things. The things some widows worry about have already been absorbed into our repertoire before the actual death. With help from my children, using their special expertise and listening ears, those big things are no longer frightening. Management is not the problem. Living is.

"How then shall we live?" On that road where there are many minefields and no guidance—all are a first time occurances. She had several suggestions from her experience: get a dog; keep busy doing the things you have always loved, travel when you want to. Coping with evenings and weekends and all that terrible aloneness—each person must find their way.

Neither of us ever considered ourselves as "dependent" types. We both had good marriages with terrific men, who knew we needed our own identity—school and work and the kind of freedom that fosters independence. Both couples preferred to work as a team but when Fran or I had opportunities to flourish on our own, we were not held back by controlling husbands. Chuck and Fritz were very much ahead of their time. They were so secure in themselves that they encouraged ambition and creativity without regard to losses they might experience.

And I suppose that I had a part in preparing that soil for growth with Fritz, as I know Fran did. Chuck was an only child and may have had his way growing up. Fritz was younger by five years than his next older brother and one of four. The brothers always knew he was spoiled as the youngest. Both Chuck and Fritz did not outwardly appear to be destined for the marriages they entered. But they thrived because we thrived.

How will this independent spirit work its way in me now that Fritz is gone? Fran couldn't tell me that. She knows that each woman has to work it out alone. Even kindred spirits can't take away the ache and replace it with joy. For many years I will be learning my own way of being a single woman.

Today I asked her the question that others are thinking but dare not ask—"would you ever consider remarrying?" No way! Was her blunt reply. Her lack of hesitation convinced me that she is still the independent woman I care about so much. Having a gentle and loving husband was once key to independence—there are no assurances that another man would provide the same.

During the last few years as Fritz's mental and physical health declined, I did what I had to do: hold things together for him and for us. Much like my mother before me, after my dad died suddenly, my first instinct is just to carry on. "We don't really have a choice," said one mother of a young child who perished in the Newtown massacre. "You deal with loss as best you can and look for new purpose in your life. The alternative is total destruction."

I may not take the same path as other widows, Fran included, but I must move along. There is no other choice. "Choose life" is the motto of a moderate pro-life movement. My life is a gift and I choose to go on living and sharing it for as many days as I am given.

4/11/13

Will I ever be able to call it mine?

I rise early on this Saturday after a rain. My first thought—I wonder how much? Before long I am out by the garden in my bathrobe checking the rain gauge. Less than a quarter inch. Not really enough to solve soil dryness, I note. The sky looks overcast so I watch for rain before turning on the water pump from the lake. I check the forecast on my cell phone.

I go out a second time with the camera to record the garden's progress and of course its beauty. This time of year, the rows look so neat filled with green foliage of different hews and heights: the spiky onions almost ready to try; the flowerets of lettuce suddenly begging to be part of my salads; the tomato plants, newly supported in their wire cages. I look across at the grapevines I so reluctantly pruned back to their bare stalks in early spring. They have taken on the shape of an African acacia tree once again, with broad leaves hiding beginning clusters of grapes. The snow peas are finally flowering, even though I got them in later than the farmer recommended.

The voice of the farmer can be heard each time I enter the enclosed garden. The warnings, the instruction of the right way, and his famous line, "can I make a suggestion?" He is still the taskmaster even though he is no longer present. His standards set a very high bar. He knew how to raise abundant

Carol tending the garden

vegetables but his "artist eye" was offended by ugliness. A garden's beauty was as important as the taste of that first strawberry or green bean.

Leonard helps me with the garden about once a week, doing the hard things like tilling the soil, spreading compost, and mending the fences. He spent last season learning under Fritz's mentoring. Between us we try to recall the instruction for each type of vegetable—often wishing the farmer could still teach or that we had listened better when he did. When the tomatoes were slower than last year, I remembered the "root blaster" which should have been sprinkled in the hole along with bone meal. Next year. Leonard recalled warnings about "bleeders," those little stems that sprout alongside the strong ones that can steal valuable nutrients from the plant. When the first potato bug began munching I ran for the "dust." It worked but I remain vigilant—can't bear to see those lush greens spoiled. I am much more willing to "thin" plants this year, knowing that the yield can actually increase if each plant has room.

I still don't know what all those sprays and insecticides in the garage cabinet should be used for. When I notice something, I survey the containers, much as I would if at Lowe's because the farmer's inventory is almost as extensive. I can hear his warning about using them carefully, as he always worried about their danger to the person who sprayed. I learned the hard way when dusting plants in a breeze and breathing in some of the same stuff that kills bugs.

It feels like midsummer when I see those nasty weeds enjoying our rich soil. It took an hour and two buckets full to clear them from a short row before planting more beans. Fritz taught me to hate weeds. I can't erase the sight of him on hands and knees meticulously weeding even when he was too weak to walk very far. His care of growing things and his vision of weed-free beauty overcame thoughts of his own comfort. Leonard has the same sensitivity; he never does anything halfway. I'm learning.

And then there are the seeds. Last year I went along with planting four varieties of carrots and five of beans to "see which one we like the best." The experiment is over. I planted one kind of each vegetable this year using seeds from last years order. They all came up.

However, I share Fritz's greed. If you can grow beautiful plants, why not grow more? If you have an empty space in a row—fill it up. If one zucchini plant produces lots, why not plant two or three? Does it take more work to plant fifteen tomatoes than six? My reality check is the memory of being challenged with too much of everything. When our tomatoes are ripe, every one else's are ripe too. Picking rows of beans in the hot sun and then hunting for people to take them came to mind even though they are the easiest to plant.

Fortunately Leonard accepted my offer to plant his Kenyan vegetables in half of the garden. The space is full but it's not all mine. He is offended when I pull his weeds. I'm happy when he pulls mine. Together we try to achieve the garden's rightful beauty. Together we try to remember all the famer's advice.

Yesterday, several friends came to photograph the blooming prairie. They were amazed that I tended the garden, knowing that Fritz was the gardener extraordinaire. We looked at it together and I felt a sense of pride. Last year I called it Fritz's garden; this year I gave him all the credit for teaching me how to grow things. I pointed out that asparagus and raspberries grow without my forethought—they are his legacy gift. At the same time, I know that each vine, plant and seedling placed in the ground this year required my labor. And I know, as Fritz did before me, that it is God who rewards the hard work.

It is my garden now. I wish it were otherwise. I wouldn't mind going back to my role as laborer and go-fer for the real farmer, even though I often complained. Following orders is much easier than giving them. My eyes feast on this garden's neat rows and weed-free beds. In time I will proudly share my produce.

But will I ever be able to call this garden mine?

The Orbit

"...darkness is banished as forward we travel from light into light.

His law he enforces; the stars in the courses; the sun in its orbit, obediently shine."

from Let All Things Now Living (written by K. Davis, 1939)

This morning I got up early and took the long walk from my house, around the block and back in a little over an hour. It is the only route I can take without retracing my steps here in the country. Mine is a walk on rural roads, up and down hills, past sour cherry and apple orchards, a wild-flower seed farm and the house where they raise birds and rabbits for sale. Most houses are hidden from view by leafy trees and tall shrubs. Completing the orbit before nine o'clock, I beat the heat and humidity of the day.

The route is familiar to me even though I have not walked it for over a year. Today marks the fourth month since Fritz died. He never walked this route with me but thought it amazing that I could. Even when he was well, his walks for pleasure were shorter and he didn't mind going out and returning the same way. He preferred hiking for a purpose like conquering a mountain in the high country or traversing fields while hunting for small game.

About this time last summer, we noticed that his orbit was getting smaller. Think of a lasso that can be pulled to a smaller and smaller circle. He didn't want me to walk with him but always told me how far he got—with a note of triumph in his voice. His steps were shorter and his gait uneven but he had incredible determination. The scientist in him still wanted to keep track, even when he sensed that his experiment was going badly.

At that time we had no explanation for his weakness and lack of stamina except the treatments. He worked while waiting, trying to feel good and do the outdoor stuff he loved. He was never one to give excuses. If a job needed doing he could not stop until it was done, no matter how badly he felt.

On that trip to Colorado last year, he staked out his orbit, from the old house up the hill to the cabin and back, pushing himself to complete it every day. He always went alone, so we couldn't see how often he stopped. Sheer determination. It is still so hard to believe he did it.

Once home, his orbit continued to shrink. Our long driveway didn't get any shorter—his distance did. By the time he got the new diagnosis of terminal cancer, he was struggling to get to the barn and back. When hospice workers began to come regularly, he often mentioned how far he had gotten on his walk. He smiled as if it were still a badge of honor. When he could no longer walk unaided he told of his forays to the front porch. One night, in the cold of winter, he got the idea that he just had to go outside. I fetched his knit cap and big down coat —it made him look twice his size. The big barrier—one step down from front door to porch; he draped himself around my shoulders as I awkwardly pulled the wheelchair to porch level. It was 10:30. He had an internal drive not to give up or give in.

In our house there was an orbit as well: bedroom to easy chair in the living room; stay for supper and TV; then back to the bedroom. I could have lain that lasso on the path and pulled it tighter as the circle got smaller. Fritz rarely came into or was curious about what went on anywhere beyond his circle. Even when his mobility gave way to a walker and then a wheelchair he went only as far as necessary.

Once he forgot about his orbit in the middle of the night. While I slept soundly, he walked into the living room until he fell beside the slider. I awoke hearing the thud. I quickly assessed that he was not injured—he had not even hit his head. Soon he stayed in the bed most of the time unless I took him for a "walk" around the house in the wheelchair. My orbit receded with his.

His final orbit was from the bed to the bathroom. Now I look at the distance and know it is incredibly short. The trip was labor intensive for both of us. Later a commode chair shortened his orbit to one step. Much too soon there was no orbit, just a one-way trip, from his bed to the hospital bed placed in the dining room.

Thoughts of Fritz come unbidden as I walk my morning circular path. I don't need the kind of determination that he had to go the distance—walking comes so easily. But once you travel the road with your husband, wife, parent or child, you know how difficult it can be. I am thankful today that I could walk every step of the way with him.

I say another word of thanks to God, knowing that I cannot take my orbit for granted. I bank my memories: the sights and sounds; the rhythm of my steps hitting the pavement; this warming, moist day of summer—treasuring life itself.

7/6/13

Sharing grief?

The invitations come each month from a local widowed persons organization offering opportunities to mingle with people who have experienced the death of a husband or wife. Other groups have been less persistent, hospice and seminars for coping with loss, but it's clear that I have entered a database of the "widowed." A friend whose wife died told me he had greatly benefited from attending two grief-groups while learning to accept life without her. Several people from my church are beginning a series called "Grief Share" this fall.

On the long road through Fritz's dementia and then cancer, I often searched for help. Being lost in new territory made me reach into places with people who were once strangers. There was so much I did not know but thought I must learn in order to survive.

The "Early Stage Dementia Group" may have been our best support group. We met with four couples in which one person had dementia. The group sessions were very concrete. I could see others trying to balance the harsh realities of Alzheimer's with efforts to preserve the dignity of the man or woman they loved. Separate sessions with the other "care partners" were more honest about feelings and concerns. We shared our fears.

When cancer became the enemy, each member of our hospice support team had a part in reassuring and guiding us through yet another minefield. We pressed for answers about the course his cancer would take, the timing of his eventual decline and when death would come. There were hints based on the experience of others but the one constant phrase, "Each person is different."

In time, death came to end Alzheimer's as well as cancer and some of our family's unknowns. Now Fritz's "case" can be added to the composite that offers very little to those who live with life-threatening illnesses. His course of life and death will always be unique; my course of living beside him is the story of only one.

On to the next stage—grief, my own foray into the unknown. I look at the brochures and the invitations that arrive. I listen to the advice of friends, trying to decide what is best for me. Not knowing what I need, I make a pile and then a folder for the file cabinet. I even put a date on the calendar of one group, which meets nearby.

Finally, I go alone to a meeting of the widowed persons' group. I walk in alongside another woman to look for the room and quickly share the facts—her husband died two months ago, mine almost six. The leaders, both widowed but now married to each other, tried to make us feel comfortable. They insisted this meeting was about sharing and encouraged dialog. Then each of us had to introduce ourselves and the particulars of our loss. Death came suddenly to some, years to others, with circumstances of tragedy or tedium, life support at a hospital or hospice care at home—all different.

The quavering of my voice surprised me as I spoke of Fritz. A few persons could hardly get past their name, their sadness so fresh or persistent.

The leaders continued tonight's topic about "Who am I now?" The topic, which drew me to the meeting in the first place, was soon nullified by a rote review of items from a manual. The leaders added a few anecdotes from their own losses but from the exuberance of their new life together. There was no discussion, for there were no questions or statements, which might have invited words from us. Another woman from the organization injected cheerleading now and then about all the activities available through their organization: cards, potlucks, golf. "So much fun—we laugh so hard." All are planned to make a space for people like me to join with those who understand.

Suddenly the hour was over and we were free to go. The woman I walked in with was seated across the room but she left before we could talk again. I spoke to several women in the parking lot but no names were exchanged. The meeting was a good idea and the leaders well-meaning, but all left me cold.

What do I need to do with my grief? I was less sure that night than I am today. I will continue to do what has worked in the past. I will write words so I can find out what I am thinking. My lifelong habit has been to get the paper when I need to dump thoughts, feelings, questions, anxieties and personal joys. As Patricia Hampl said so wisely, "We do not, after all, simply have experience—we are entrusted with it. We must do something—make something—with it. A story, we sense, is the only possible *habitation* for the burden of our witnessing."

I have my journal for the first dumping. Then as feelings intensify and clarify I need to write more—a personal essay, a chunk of memoir, sometimes a poem. Tell the story, my story in a way that defies chitchat with people thrown together because of loss. Against all advice, I need to be alone—to think, to feel and to write. I cannot isolate myself all the time, but I sense that healing, if it is to come, will happen in the quiet of my room, sitting at my desk, typing away in search of words to say what is in my mind.

Carol (young) holding picture of Fritz

The agony of Fritz's loss began when he could not find words to tell me what he was thinking. Lost were the names of people and names of his beloved vegetables and then ideas that brought meaning to his days. Without language, description is lost, longings cannot be expressed, order cannot return. Today I still have words. I must build a home, a habitation for all I have experienced in my life, brick by brick—with words. Grief will make up many bricks. I'm building one story at a time. Someday I might reach the rooftop.

8/31/13

Marking Time

No need to mark the calendar
loss keeps its own time
How long?
so long
too long—alone.

Months measure time
since his life ended.
Each has a day 2,
now nine since March.

Timeless love suspended in time,
'til the calendar reaches 2—
the pause-button releases
animates loss again.

Time stopped for him
one chilly day in Spring.
For me, marking time began, unbidden,
living out distance from that day.

When twelve months pass
can I move ahead to years?
Dry my eyes
only year to year?

The day we met,
the day we wed,
a new anniversary:
the day we parted.

C. Rottman, 12/2/13

Many Random Pieces

The stores called to me two days after Christmas. I have never been much of a shopper but got restless in the aftermath of holiday busyness. No gifts to return, just a short list of little things to look for. Knowing that the Christmas tree, which filled my dining room would soon be "out of season" and dry as kindling, I thought I'd try a craft store for something decorative. In comparison to a living tree, the fare looked pretty tawdry. So I followed the signs to after Christmas sales—sixty percent off. A couple of red ornaments, a large silver bow and two boxes of tree lights amounted to less than five dollars. On the way to checkout, the puzzle display caught my eye.

Puzzles for me are like magnets. Can't walk by one in progress without laying my hand on a piece. After Thanksgiving I decided to finish one the grandchildren had started only to discover that each piece had many iterations of shape and could be laid in a number of places. The picture was of the familiar Dead Horse Mill in Colorado, which in itself was hard to resist. Each home in our family has a similar picture of this ancient mill up-mountain from Marble—one of our favorite places. I gave the little miniature puzzle way too much time, squinting to find the variations in color and shade. Days later it was finished; I went to bed congratulating myself for stick-to-it-tive-ness, if not satisfaction. But in the light of day, I discovered that the picture was not right—the wall of the mill was not straight, the trees separated from their roots. I frantically switched pieces until it was a hopeless jumble. In a fit of despair I took the whole thing and threw it in the trash.

A few days later I went to my daughter's for an evening. The five people there for Christmas started a polar bear/Coke puzzle that was supposed to look like that ad on TV—a sea of white fir on an ice float and a couple bottles of Coke. Each of the bottles was completed but not attached. I was not alone in being unable to find one fit after twenty minutes of staring at the huge unmarked expanse. I expect the fate of this one may be similar to that of the mill.

At the store I walked around the puzzle display table several times. I wanted one. My puzzle craving had to be satisfied. Based on my recent history, it must have pieces of unique shapes, contrasting in color and detail, to make up for my color deficits. I must have handled every box—eliminating many. Finally one called out to me: multiple canning jars on a shelf full of fruit and surrounded by containers like colanders and baskets of more fruit. I hesitated for one minute at the number of pieces, 1000. I never looked at the area size. When it rang up at sixteen dollars I almost reneged, but by then I had to have it.

This puzzle had everything including size—enough to fill my whole round kitchen table. I left the red Christmas

The Puzzle

cloth on the table as I began finding the side pieces and knitting them together. There was little room to put other pieces on the outside so I filled the center with one color or pattern at a time. Again I launched into a four-day obsession. This one met every requirement; I would not let it beat me. A few people came by and lent a hand. "That is really big, Grandma!" Even folks stymied by the polar bear, left saying, "Better than that one but still hard!"

Ever since my husband died ten months ago, the hardest thing has been to endure long evenings or those times after guests go home. I have dabbled with Ruzzle on my phone and Scrabble on my Kindle for the quick challenge. I left each as I felt the addiction factor taking over. I didn't care if I won or lost—just had to keep going through the motions. I am often too restless to get lost in a novel. So the puzzle seemed to be a wholesome alternative. There would be a beginning and an end. Sometime—there would be an end.

One challenge was seeing the pieces. When I had pared down the thousand a bit, I laid the others on every surface in the kitchen, including several baking trays that could be stacked or moved. I could not see well from a sitting position so I stood and walked around the table repeatedly in search of a match for a quirky space. The red background of the tablecloth certainly threw me off. Sometimes I worked on it so long my legs ached and my eyes were bleary. I forgot to eat. I fell into bed exhausted. Next day when I got breakfast, I turned my back to the puzzle so as not to get drawn back by the siren call. Finally I used the puzzle as a short reward after some real work, by setting the kitchen timer for a fifteen-minute session. I know about Pavlov.

One part of your brain works with puzzles; another part ponders just why you are doing this to yourself—setting up a challenge that seems almost insurmountable. While the hands and eyes do their thing to fill an artificial frame, the other part longs to be comforted by a sense of meaning. Before beginning you hardly question. During the process you learn something about yourself. At the end, you really wonder why.

I suspect one part of me loves to see disorder turn into order. That pile of random pieces, some with only the gray backside showing is the picture of chaos. The longer you stay with it, the more organized it becomes. The jars of fruit fill and the shining tops are screwed on, each with a piece of fabric between the two parts of the lid. The colander of strawberries

Doug and parents in Marble

is washed and ready to serve. Two kitchen towels hang ready to use. Tin cans of fruit regain their labels.

Am I searching for that kind of order? Puzzle pieces fix broken pictures; this one preserves jars of fruit to be used during the long winter. Puzzles restore the belief that chaos will find its own synchrony. The photograph I took of the finished product while standing on a chair with my camera poised above it is a lasting image.

My daughter dropped by today. I displayed the puzzle with some pride, saying I kept it just long enough for her to see. She believed me, found the box and began taking all 1,000 pieces apart so no two remained attached. If she had not come, who knows how long I would have hung on to that orderly picture as a reminder that the broken can be put back together.

Now here I am, for the first time in weeks, bringing some kind of order to the randomness of my life by writing. Words on a page start as a puzzle too—not knowing where they will land. Will they have color and nuance that sets them apart as unique? Will they become a beautiful picture? Even when life changes will the memory of beautiful order linger in my mind?

I have a thousand pieces stowed in a box that say it will.

C. Rottman, 1/4/14

Reflection

Early this morning as Doug and I made our way to East Lansing, a car went out of control about one hundred yards ahead of us. With his help I navigated the van safely through the danger. I still see the careening car cross from the left-side bank directly across and crash head on into the guardrail. I am still shaking; it is hard to erase that visual from my mind.

None of us knows when our end will come. I'm praying for more days and years. This morning I witnessed potential tragedy; I know that all moments are gifts. So today I want to claim a full life even as a single woman, knowing how fragile life is.

Fritz, my precious encourager will be proud if I can use the gifts God gave me, and go on living. At important junctures in our long marriage, he gave me the nudge I needed. "You can do that," he'd say, never doubting for a moment. As he was dying, he rested peacefully in the belief that I had what it would take to carry on without him.

When in doubt—I'll wait for that nudge. I can feel it now.

The End

Mysterious, illusive, unknown
  'til it comes
Withered coneflowers of the field
  Doe petrified in head-lights
    A planet run its course.

Some long to find comfort
in knowing when
  until without foresight
Embracing the end.

Like beginnings—no time before time
No glimpse beyond the great divide,
No knowledge before seeing face to face.

Year's end ushers year's beginning
Hardly time to say good-bye
As I must one day
To this land, these sticks of trees, this frozen earth.

Goodbye—before my last breath
To my wild dreamer—
To the flowers of friendship
Of children, finches and swans
Bluestem and lupine.

Spring rains—bless blooms for new eyes
Waving grass—stir other hearts
  Mere words recount life as pilgrimage
    Long after our quest is won.

Carol J. Rottman,
adapted from a poem in All Nature Sings:
A Spiritual Memoir of Place

The wildflowers continue to bloom

> *Precious Lord, take my hand*
> *Lead me on, let me stand*
> *I'm tired, I'm weak, I'm lone*
> *Through the storm, through the night*
> *Lead me on to the light*
> *Take my hand precious Lord, lead me home*

Dorsey

ACKNOWLEDGEMENTS

A book never grows up alone in the author's mind, especially one of memoir. While the experiences in this screenplay were seen through the author's eyes alone, there was a large supporting cast that brought the story to life. If this were a movie the credits might run like this:

Producer: Dirk Wierenga

Editorial Staff: Principia staff and consultants

Photographic Restoration: Sherry Baribeau

Artistic Director: Frank Gutbord

Lead Actor: Fritz Rottman

Supporting Cast: the Rottman family

Technical Assistants: Hospice of Grand Rapids, Compassionate Physicians

The Cloud of witnesses: Members of Eastern Avenue Christian Reformed Church

Plot Design: Journey Group: Writing as an Act of Faith

Quality Control: Grand Rapids Writer's group

Crowds of onlookers:

Writing students in Calvin Academy for Livelong Learning

Filming location: Greenville, Michigan and Marble, Colorado

To all of you artists listed above, doing the work you were called to by God and who generously gave of your talents in support of this book, I shout out my sincere thanks.

Carol J. Rottman

About the Cover:

Orchids are "beauty in symmetry," a silent message of love and affection. Two blossoms in close proximity like a marriage of equals built on a sturdy stalk, long-lasting though fragile as life itself.

BIO

Carol Rottman writes memoir and teaches creative non-fiction in Grand Rapids, Michigan. Her roots are in Denver but she migrated to Michigan for college and settled there with her husband, Fritz. After careers in teaching young blind children, managing an inner-city program for women and a technical writing business, Carol concentrated on creative non-fiction.

Carol says, "I love writing short personal essays that I call "chunks of memoir." They can either stand alone or in clusters to form a Memoir. When teaching older adults in the *Telling Your Stories: Creating Memoir* course, I urge them to do the same when writing about their long and colorful lives. Together we hone our story-telling skills on the page so our stories will not be lost to the next generation."

Carol began by writing collections of meditations, *Mountain Meditations* and *Clouds: Big with Mercy* and *Kenya to New Eyes* to share with friends. After taking classes for a dozen summers at the Iowa Summer Writing Festival, she had amassed a number of personal essays, many about being a fledgling writer. At the suggestion of a friend, she gathered them into her first book of memoir, *Writers in the Spirit: Inspiration for Christian Writers* (2004), which she uses as the textbook in her classes. *All Nature Sings: A Spiritual Journey of Place* (2010) is a memoir written after moving from the city (Cleveland) to the country (Greenville, Mi.) where she and her husband restored a native prairie. *A Memoir of Parting* (2016) was written during their last three years together.

Her three children, spouses and eight adult grandchildren continue to enrich her life. With them in mind, she is writing the stories of over sixty years of returning to a little cabin in Marble, Colorado, where each of them has come since infancy. The running title for the new collection is: *Places of the Heart: Mountain Rocks.*

BOOKS BY
CAROL ROTTMAN

All Nature Sings: A Spiritual Journey of Place
(2010, Credo House Publishers)
ISBN-10: 1-935391-40-2,
ISBN-13: 978-1-935391-40-1

Writers in the Spirit: Inspiration for Christian Writers
(2004, Faith Walk Publishing)
ISBN-10: 1-932902-43-0,
ISBN-13: 978-1-932902-43-3